Troubled Traveler
A Young Man's Odyssey Through Mexico

John Gernandt

Copyright © 2024 John Gernandt

All rights reserved. No part of this book may be reproduced or transmitted in any form or by any means, electronic or mechanical, including photocopying, recording or by any information storage and retrieval system without permission in writing from the publisher.

Milpas Press—Fitchburg, WI
ISBN: 979-8-218-40373-7
Library of Congress Control Number: 2024912062
Title: *Troubled Traveler: A Young Man's Odyssey Through Mexico*
Author: John Gernandt
Digital distribution | 2024
Paperback | 2024

Published in the United States by New Book Authors Publishing

Dedication

To my wife, Suzanne, my best friend, my greatest supporter, and my guide through the book writing process. And, to the friends and family who have heard some of these stories and encouraged me to write them down.

Table of Contents

Part One 1
Chapter 1: Landing in Mexico 2
Chapter 2: Leaving Mexico City 9
Chapter 3: Bush Mission with Uncle Bill 23
Chapter 4: New Friends – Back in Jalapa 33
Chapter 5: A Visit Home 55
Part Two..61
Chapter 6: Heading Back Through Nogales 63
Chapter 7: The Monkey and Me 75
Chapter 8: Side Trip to Zongolica 79
Chapter 9: To Oaxaca 85
Chapter 10: The Land of Magic Mushrooms..........91
Chapter 11: Off to an Island 97
Chapter 12: Finally Heading to Sitala 105
Part Three..115
Chapter 13: Arrived in Sitala 117
Chapter 14: The Clinic..127
Chapter 15: Yajalon, Bachajon and Chilon 141
Chapter 16: Coffee Harvest....................................157
Chapter 17: Padre "A" and Birth Certificates.......163
Chapter 18: Planning to Exit the Highlands 171
Part Four 179
Chapter 19: Back in the USA 181
Chapter 20: UCLA or not?......................................187
Chapter 21: The Hospital and Testing 193
Chapter 22: The Surgery..207
Epilogue...217

MAYA NUMERALS

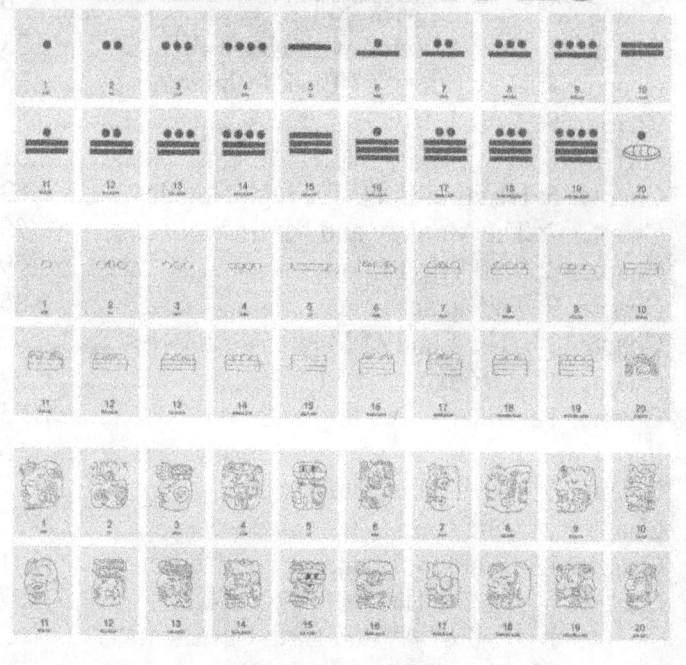

"It's how you handle adversity, not how it affects you. The main thing is never quit, never quit, never quit."

— Bill Clinton

Part One

Chapter 1

Landing in Mexico

I guess I'm ready. My parents drive me to LAX and put me on a plane headed to Mexico City. My mom hugging me, trying not to cry, acting strong for my sake. My dad, in his business suit, seems emotionless, but he gives me a hug. Alone, barely sixteen years old with minimal Spanish, and there will be no one to meet me at the airport. I can do it. During the flight over the Sonoran Desert and the inland states of Mexico, I see the Chihuahua mountains rise out of the desert and the green valleys and lakes surrounding Guadalajara and the state of Jalisco. This gives me a hint of the land I will soon be exploring. We circle the tall mountains surrounding the valley where Mexico City awaits me and begin our descent into this metropolis of eleven million people in an area smaller than New York City. I am both jumping inside with anticipation and trembling with fear.

I get off the plane and enter a building full of frenzied people going in every direction. All the signs are in Spanish, none of which I can read, except for an occasional word. Unfamiliar odors fill the air, not unpleasant smells, but unlike any I have smelled before. What comes to my mind is the translation of the word "chaos" in Chinese, two words "Danger = Opportunity." The math required to change dollars to pesos confuses me and I end up at a kiosk where, for a fee, they calculate the exchange. Food is everywhere, and I am ravenous. All manner of foodstuff is spread out on the floor, on top of blankets, in buckets, crates and on primitive shelving. Menus or descriptions are nonexistent. You point or call out for what you want from the many choices available. I go for the tamales. I know what they are. Mothers of the Mexican students in my elementary school brought them for lunch one day each week. All the stories about the health dangers of eating and drinking in a foreign country are bouncing in my head, but I am famished and have to eat something.

After I eat and settle down a little, I take a deep breath and pull a piece of paper from my pocket containing directions to the city of Jalapa, the capital of the state of Veracruz, and my final destination.

Why Jalapa? My Uncle Bill, a Jesuit Catholic missionary assigned to Jalapa, lives and works there. A great guy, my mother's brother, someone we all look up to, a priest, an Olympic swimming and boxing coach, a previous chaplain at Alcatraz prison. He will be the starting point in my journey to become someone other than a kid known as trouble.

I wander out of the airport to a chaos of cars and buses everywhere, people yelling and signs I do not understand. Finally, I find someone who speaks a little English, and with a bit of sign language he understands that I want to go to the bus station to buy a ticket. Via taxi, I find my way to the ADO, the equivalent of a

Greyhound station. The agents speak English, and when I describe where I'm going, I learn the next bus will leave the following day at 10:00 AM.

At the bus station, I am fascinated by the people, their clothing, and all the food everywhere. Fresh fruits, vegetables, nuts and seeds, and numerous snacks and finger foods. So many small kiosks are scattered throughout the station that I don't know where to start. The languages and behaviors are so different from what I am accustomed to in Southern California, where everyone looks, smells, speaks, eats, and behaves the same. More so than in the airport, the bus terminal drops me into another world. I know what Spanish sounds like, but I'm hearing more than sixty indigenous languages, root dialects of Mayan, Aztec and Nahuatl cultures. I love everything I see and hear. The streets are alive with people wearing indigenous clothing in the most vivid colors and designs.

I am struck by the kindness people show one another. The people begging and seeking help in the street are given both resources and respect. People greet each other when passing, "Adios, Adios." The poor are handing out money and food to those who are more disadvantaged than themselves. I am seeing a living example of people being treated equally. The day before, I was seeing the opposite – racial discrimination across America.

What to do? I need to find a safe place to sleep, and fear is setting in. Plus, I'm tired from the five-hour flight and the confusion at the airport and bus station. Okay, I will find an affordable place for the night. Downtown Mexico City is expensive and has many large tourist and business hotels, like places my family might stay when on vacation. But I'm not on vacation, I'm all alone. I don't know if anyone will rent a room to a sixteen-year-old without identification, and no credit card. Of course, in 1968, nobody had a credit card, and I had $500 in American Express Travelers Checks. I hope I won't be sleeping on the street. Giving up and failing in the first twenty-four hours of my new life is not an option, I need a short-term plan. I can't read Spanish, so hotel brochures will not work. Taxi drivers and people on the street don't speak English.

My idea is to get help from a hotel concierge who speaks English at one of the big hotels. I tuck in my shirt and pull back my hair, thinking I look pretty darn good, maybe even almost like a grown-up. Feeling pleased with myself, I try a few hotels, but no one speaks English. Finally, I meet someone who has visited San Diego and speaks English. She is dressed professionally, but is friendly and not hesitant to help. We talk a bit and she refers me to the Hotel Jena. She writes out directions, and I take off on foot. Now it is becoming dark and the street signs are hard to read. Crowds of people fill the streets. I walk for several minutes, turn the corner, and there stands the Hotel Jena, a five-story hotel not far from downtown. Rooms are only ten dollars a night. I have no problem checking in. They don't bat an eye at my age or my long, curly, red hair. I receive a key and a slip of paper explaining the check-out procedure and a few other things, all in English.

When I get to my room, on the fifth floor, the window is open to the street. It's loud. I hear yelling and what sounds like gunfire. The 1968 Olympics are in Mexico City this year, which explains the sizeable crowds on the streets. Looking down, I see a large group of people coming up the middle of the road, protesting some aspect of the Olympics. Moving toward them are men dressed in military uniforms, carrying weapons and yelling at the people to get off the street and move to the sidewalk. I don't understand their words, but it is apparent, even from my window, that there is not enough room on the sidewalk for all the people in the street. In the mass confusion, suddenly, the uniformed men start to shoot anyone unable to get onto the sidewalk. Men, women and children are being shot and killed right outside my hotel window. Having lived close to Los Angeles during the 1965 race riots, I know that things like this happen, but they are not supposed to happen in front of me. I long, in that moment, for an adult to tell me what I am seeing, to comfort and console me. I hunker down in my room for several hours, away from the windows, trying to be safe. It occurs to me that this morning I was a sixteen-year-old boy with his parents. Now I am that same kid, but watching people die in front of me. How could this be happening?

By late evening, I'm hungrier than ever, and nothing is going to stop me from venturing down to the first floor for food. Should I take the fire exit down the concrete stairs or the elevator straight to the lobby, like normal people? I want the safest route, no matter what. Several hours have passed since the shootings, and on the street, the fire trucks, police ambulances, and tear gas are beginning to thin out. I make it to the street, where it looks safe enough, but smells terrible, like burnt hair, gunpowder and spent tear gas. I spot a man selling what looks like pancakes from a pushcart with a small griddle on top where he cooks a pancake, and reaches over to a pan of warm caramelized, sweetened, and condensed milk, which he ladles onto the pancake. Finally, he rolls it up and hands it to me with a napkin. On the side of the cart are bowls of powdered sugar, jams, and fresh fruits and berries. It is so delicious that I have several more. Finally, a full belly.

When I return to the hotel, it is still night. People are cleaning up the broken glass, blood and clothing scattered on the street. So many beautiful sights and things to see in Mexico City, yet I have only seen the worst. I sit anxiously in my room waiting for morning, and the bus ride to Jalapa. I am sickened by what I witnessed earlier, too afraid to think about what the next day might bring. This city is so big, with so many people I can't communicate with, except through attempts at sign language. After a bit of restless sleep, I walk to the bus station as dawn is breaking, figuring I might as well be there as anywhere else, even though I feel like I am sitting there like a homeless teenager, with no destination, and people staring at me.

After an hour on the wooden bench waiting for the bus, I begin to relax and think that being a stranger in a strange place isn't so bad after all. I know no one. I have a blank slate. I can be anyone I want. I don't have to be the bad boy anymore. I am a fresh face. Feeling better, I sit up straight and think: screw everyone. You don't even know me. You cannot think bad things about me.

Chapter 2

Leaving Mexico City

The bus ride to Jalapa is five hours. People board the bus with their children, musical instruments, pets, and food packed in colorful bags. During the trip, they all talk to each other, play music and sing, with children playing in the aisle and food shared among everyone. The entire atmosphere feels like a party, with everyone enjoying the trip.

There is so much to look at, and absorb, that time goes by quickly. After we leave the city, the landscape becomes more rural, with a lot of activity along the sides of the highway. People lead donkeys, and oxen pull carts full of fresh produce. Many people and families are walking, taking their cows, pigs, goats, and chickens to the local markets. As we leave the valley of Mexico City, looking to the northwest, I see what I will later learn is Popocatepetl, the mountain range containing three peaks, resembling a sleeping woman, snowcapped almost year-round. Popocatepetl is a volcano, the second highest peak in Mexico at 17,887 feet. The locals affectionately shorten the name Popocatepetl, Aztec for Smoking Mountain, to Popo. The further east we travel, towards the center of the state of Puebla, the landscape becomes sparser yet.

After several hours, we arrive at the large city of Puebla for a two-hour layover, and I'm delighted to see there is a celebration and fiesta happening in the town square. I am fascinated by the many indigenous people coming into town, on foot or on the Fleche Roja, the second-class bus, or by donkey carts and cars. People's clothing colors and styles represent different regions, and it's easy to differentiate the city dwellers from the rural.

I spend a long time studying both the interior and exterior of the cathedral in the center of town. Never have I seen a building so full of intricate detail and splendid beauty. Somehow, I know intuitively that people living in that region made all the woodcarving and plaster ornamentation by hand. Both primitive and finely crafted churches are everywhere throughout the city, each one named for a different Catholic Saint. I pick up a brochure in English and learn that there is a church for each day of the year in Puebla, three hundred and sixty-five of them, all used daily. Puebloans take a lot of pride in their city; it is here, in Puebla, that Mexico gained independence from the French in 1821.

Back on the bus, next stop: Jalapa, Veracruz. Driving out of Puebla, we climb in elevation. As we get closer to Jalapa, the vegetation changes and we are in a high, semi-tropical area, with humid forests and dense undergrowth. Coffee ranches, agriculture, dairy, and poultry farms surround the hillsides.

As I step off the bus and look around, I don't know what to expect. I hope Uncle Bill will be there to meet me, but if not, I'm ready to deal with any challenges that may lie ahead. Thankfully, the Jalapa bus station is much less confusing than the bus terminal in Mexico City. The weather is chippy-chippy, a local word for the wet, heavy fog that is common here.

I stand still as a statue, waiting to see someone or hear a familiar voice. Then I hear a loud, memorable voice and there is my Uncle Bill, a large man with a big, happy Irish smile. That big smile is so comforting. I feel safe for the first time since the plane landed. Uncle Bill is as relieved to see me as I am to see him. Knowing what happened in Mexico City the night before, he's been worried about me. At a nearby coffee shop, we talk about the violence. I'm not sure it's reassuring when he points out had I arrived at the hotel a few hours later, someone could have shot me just for being in the street. Later, I learn that altogether, the police and soldiers shot 350-400 protesters and innocent people on the street in the 1968 Olympic Tlatelolco Massacre.

As we chat, I learn that I won't be staying with Uncle Bill at the church rectory after all. I'll be staying at the house of a Catholic nun named Lucy who is also a CPA, whatever that is. She owns a large home, which she shares with her two aunts, two nieces and one nephew. This news feels like a body blow, but I have no choice but to agree, since the decision has clearly already been made.

This Lucy and her family will be my new family. I will have to be on my best behavior. I can't screw up. I am filled with questions I don't know how to ask, my mind racing as we sit drinking our coffee. How will they understand me? Do they know about my past?

Can I fake it and lie if they ask questions? What should I do? I reach out to Bill for answers. I want him to know how scared and uncertain I feel. My vulnerability hovers right on the surface. How can I explain to this Lucy why I am there? I'll be living with three teenagers, all older than me, who speak a language foreign to me. These are the people who will be my gateway to this new community. Will I spoil it? I desperately want to be successful in this new environment. I have messed up so badly at home, and I'm still not at all sure why or what exactly went wrong. Will it work? Can I handle it? All I can do is try.

Driving through downtown Jalapa with Uncle Bill calms me down. I'm impressed, not only by the cleanliness of the city, but by its beautiful architecture, its many public gardens, and the bustling urban environment. Both a government town and a big university town, with a few smaller colleges and museums, it has open markets, parks, fountains, and the traditional large town square. The downtown streets are filled with buses, cars, scooters, people of all ages, and street vendors everywhere selling anything and everything - breads, juices, pancakes, tacos, fruit, candy, chickens, both alive and dead. We pass shoeshine stations, and sidewalk pharmacies displaying everything from antibiotics to Indian herbs. You can buy a pig or a goat on the sidewalk or even get a haircut. You name it, someone is selling it. The more we drive, the more the city streets resemble the steep streets of San Francisco.

After our tour, I grab my backpack from the car, and

we head off on foot to Lucy's, about eight blocks away. We walk south away from town to a district known as the Dique, or the Dike; the name has something to do with a small river. Down a narrow street we come to a yellow concrete house, address Calle 57, that fronts a busy sidewalk. The architectural style is unfamiliar to me. The house is built next to the sidewalk, the large open windows of the kitchen and laundry room facing outwards. It looks awkward but is a typical design for Jalapa. We knock and enter a charming, well-designed interior.

By now, I am tremendously nervous again and feel like throwing up. Bill introduces me to Lucy, a short, stocky woman in her middle thirties, I guess, dressed in business style. Lucy introduces me to Tia and Teta, her two aunts. They seem old to me, older than Uncle Bill or my parents, maybe in their mid-forties, and they seem in control of the house and kitchen. Next, the teenagers: Margarita, the oldest girl; Jose, the only boy; and Lupe, the youngest girl, closest to my age. None of them shows any interest in me. I am a complete interruption from their daily lives. Margarita, Jose, and Lupe are all in college, busy with friends and their own lives. Tia and Teta give me the little evil eye. Like, who are you to enter our home?

Everyone is nice and polite, but the language barrier is awkward, and I know I will have to work that out. No one in the family speaks a word of English and as the guest in their home and their country, the burden is on me. I must learn Spanish quickly. Margarita, Lupe, and Jose excuse themselves and leave the room. Lucy shows me to the room I will share with Jose, a masonry block space off the side of the kitchen. Two twin beds, two nightstands, two dressers and bed lights, and tiled floors. I put my clothes away and venture back into the main house. Lucy is waiting for me, ready to set out tea and cookies. She invites me to sit and share pictures of my family. Soon, Margarita comes in and joins us. She is shy and sits with the left side of her body hidden from me. Even so, I notice she has a prosthetic left arm, an inexpensive model made of flexible rubber, typical in Mexico, a cosmetic device with no actual function. I am not bothered by her arm and wish she weren't so self-conscious about it.

Uncle Bill returns at dinner time. I am starving again because they do not serve dinner in Mexico until late, 7 or 8 o'clock. It's not a full dinner either, more of a snack. The larger meal is served at lunch. I am the only one at the table with no place setting. I think Uncle Bill planned this with Lucy. Everyone sits down and Uncle Bill says, "John, if you want silverware, you are going to ask for it."

Okay, my first Spanish lesson. Bill and the whole family take part in my learning and humiliation. Tenedor (fork), cuchillo (knife), cuchara (spoon) and so on. This will continue at every meal until I have it down. Then we move on to food and drink. I will have to learn these words or go hungry.

I meet every day with the Spanish tutor Uncle Bill hired, and I improve rapidly in just a few weeks. Most days I walk downtown to the local coffee shop. They serve the best coffee I've ever tasted, from Coatepec, the coffee and vanilla capital of Mexico, just a few miles from Jalapa. Cafe con leche is my favorite, with fresh vanilla shavings on top. There is a Language Institute at the university, with international students from England, France, and all over the world. I meet several American students from the east coast, and we become casual friends, frequently meeting up for coffee together, even though I often feel out of place because they are actual students, and I am just hanging out. They are studying Spanish literature, and I'm just trying my best to learn Spanish. As much as I want to fit in, I know I don't. Everything that has led me to Mexico is so deeply personal and is such a muddle in my mind. I'm not ready to share my story with anyone, and I find myself sitting silently as they chatter away, my mind drifting back to earlier days.

I had behavioral problems as early as kindergarten. I remember sitting for hours in a hard wood chair in a dingy, windowless room in the back of the classroom, staring at the gray vinyl floor. Meanwhile, my classmates were playing, eating lunch, or watching a movie. Maybe I was rough with the other children, talking mean, or teasing others, I don't know. Maybe I forgot the teacher's instructions, or I could not comprehend what was going on in the classroom. I don't know that either. I know I was always being placed in that room with the gray vinyl floor, away from the others. The teacher may have told me I did something wrong, but all I remember is the teacher saying, "I will have to tell your parents about this."

These words terrified me because the results were always the same. I would come home from school, and

I would be told to go upstairs and wait for my father. When he arrived, he'd tell me to pull down my pants. Then he'd remove his belt and spank me. Worse than being hit was having to stay in my room and think about what I had done while I could hear my brothers having fun downstairs. I'd cry louder and louder until my mother came up the stairs to comfort me and assure me everything would be all right. Mom would negotiate with my dad for my return to the family. Back then she was always my savior. I understand my father had had a rough time as an only child and lacked a role model for being a compassionate father. I observed that many times my grandmother would call in a panic, asking my father to come over right away, because my grandfather was out of control, tearing up the house and breaking things. With us, his grandchildren, his discipline bordered on abuse. My sister was afraid to be in a room alone with him. Much later I learned that my grandfather suffered from an undiagnosed mental illness.

I suppose I was a lucky kid, since we lived in an upper middle class Los Angeles suburb we referred to as "Vatican Hill," filled with big houses and large Catholic families. We rode our bikes, played flag football, and hung out in the neighborhood. I was the boy with more behavior problems than anyone else.

As a young child. I was always in trouble, nothing unlawful, not fighting or stealing. Somehow, I seemed to always do the wrong thing and get punished for it, both physically beaten and shamed. I was constantly being told to shape up, be a good boy. Why are you doing what you're doing? I don't think I realized I had broken something, or used swear words, or been disobedient or disrespectful. One day when I was five years old and feeling misunderstood and unloved by my parents, I staged my death in the driveway with a knife and a bottle of ketchup. I was not thinking about suicide. My stunt was a child's way of reaching out for understanding. Once again, my actions were misunderstood and punished. My early childhood continued this downward path. I did not understand what was going on and I suspected I was different from my brothers and the other neighborhood kids. Not until I was around eleven years old did teachers, doctors, and my parents realize I didn't comprehend my own behavior or others response to it. My parents followed the advice of teachers and counselors to seek professional help. Testing showed that I was smart and should be doing better in school. My parents and counselors thought I would grow out of this difficult phase, but I never did. My behavior just deteriorated.

The first few weeks in Jalapa, I call home every week. In 1968, this is a real ordeal. Long distance anywhere, but especially to another country, takes some time and money. I talk to my mom and dad to convince them I am okay and comfortable at Lucy's. Mom, always reassuring, continually expresses her love and encouragement. Dad, on the other hand, seems to think that the mere act of leaving home has cured me. He seems to be only concerned about the expensive phone calls; if he could quit sending me money now, perhaps I could live in Mexico forever? I wanted to say hi to my brothers and my sister, but Dad would end the call before I could ask. Trying to save Dad's money, I started sending picture postcards instead of calling. I know they enjoyed seeing the picture postcards, and it was at least a visual way of staying in touch with my siblings.

I see my new friends less often. They are in class studying or hanging out, and I feel more uncomfortable around them as time goes on. I spend my days walking the streets and trying to understand everything I see. I love how different everything looks and tastes and smells and sounds. So many people with very little money, but their lives are so rich. Friendly people are everywhere, smiling and greeting one another "Hola" or "Adios." I receive a hundred Adios on one city block. I'm still astonished by the quantity and varieties of food available. No one is going hungry. If you need food, someone will give you some. I buy an apple on the street one day; the vendor says if I am hungry to take two. On every corner something is cooking. One of my favorites is mango on a stick. The cost, un peso, around ten cents, and it tastes like a million dollars. I quickly learn to limit my street eating or it will interfere with the big lunch waiting for me at Lucy's.

In Mexico, families gather at mid-day for the main meal. The kitchen is busy, a large pot of beans always simmering on the stove. The smells are mouthwatering. At Lucy's, the kitchen is at the back of the house, parallel to the sidewalk with a large opening in the wall that faces the street. This opening serves as access for all the vendors to advertise their goods and services, calling them out as they walk past the house. It is exciting to hear them when they come by. Pollo (chicken), pan (bread), leche (milk), fruta (fruit), and cuchillos (knives). The el afilador–knife sharpener blows a whistle, a distinctive sound that everyone knows. He pushes his cart with its large stone wheel down the sidewalk. It's a great service. If you need a knife sharpened, listen for the whistle, hand the knife out the window, and the job is done. Another treat is the kitchen cookware and accessories street vendors pushing their overcrowded carts up and down the street, shouting out the goods they carry. They have everything: pots and pans, colanders, silverware, plates, glasses and all the native Mexican cookware. I often stop the vendor of utensilios to ask questions and learn new vocabulary words.

At meals, the table is now set without my having to ask for dinner ware. I must have passed the test. After everyone is seated, we share events of our day. Still self-conscious and uncomfortable with my Spanish, I do the best I can to share my excitement about all I have seen each day. After several months, I think the family is getting bored with my experiences. Nonetheless, I appreciate all the help I am getting with Spanish.

My favorite dish: enchiladas de pollo con mole negro con arroz, (chicken enchiladas with black mole and rice), topped off with traditional queso, or cheese. Unlike the red mole served in Northern Mexico, this is black mole made with over 32 seasonings. It tastes rich, a layered, earthy taste with a bold chocolate, coffee, and bean flavor. Tortillas are a staple always on the table, along with a plate of assorted fruit. I am so impressed with the mole that one afternoon, I go back to the market to see how it is sold. After a ten-minute walk to the market dodging carts, baskets and people, I arrive at the spice area of the market. After asking a few questions, I find the black mole and am surprised to see it displayed as a brick. It is sold by the kilo and melted down to create the sauce. I have a great, though challenging conversation with the vendor who speaks very little Spanish, but a dialect I don't know at all. I kept forgetting that in the southern half of Mexico, a third of the people speak Indian dialects derived from Aztec and Mayan languages. She explains that most of the black mole comes from a region a day away from Jalapa. It is a slow, very complex process, with many spices being added at different times as it cooks. The mole cooks down to a thick paste consistency, and is then put into a mold, where it cools and dries for weeks. The time and care it takes is worth the flavor. To this day, anything with black mole sauce is one of my favorite foods.

    On a typical day, after lunch, I walk back downtown to explore. One day I change my route, making it a little longer, and find myself in a place where many service workers hang out. Plumbers, electricians, carpenters, and movers. The cargaderos (movers) are the most unique. These guys are human U-Haul trucks. They carry everything on their backs. I sit and talk with them for quite a while. I'm particularly drawn to Juanote (Big John), an enormous, silent, Zen-like man. Juanote tells me he grew up in Tabasco, a city south of Veracruz and helped his mom carry firewood, water, and sugar cane and trained for many years to carry heavy cargo. He moves appliances for a local store. When something large needs to be moved, a young girl, the daughter of the store manager, runs down the street to tell Juanote. He gathers his leather strap that fits over his forehead and goes to work. I watch him squat down, rest a refrigerator on his back and carry it off, up and down the steep streets. I mention this to someone later who says, "Oh yeah, that must have been Juanote, the cargadero. He's well known in town for moving the big stuff." Juanote and I become friends and always greet each other on the street. I call out Hola, Juanote and he calls back, Hola Juan Colorado (John of the color red.)

The carpenters I see make me think about my grandfather. An architect and carpenter, he worked at a large old drafting table, which I still use today. His drawings were all done in pencil with incredible detail. He would draw not only the structure of the home he was designing, but the design and every detail of the wrought iron stairs, banisters, and handrails. He shared with me the drawings he did when he designed the Jai Alai stadium in Havana, Cuba. In pencil, he drew every detail of the artful plaster ornamentation on the walls and ceilings. I was told that he was a real hands-on architect working with each artisan on the trades they were working on. My grandfather described how he could identify the trade of any man by the toolbox they were carrying. Here in Mexico, I observe that men working the trades seem to be easygoing, contemplative, and serious about their work, unlike the men working in the market or vendors on the street, who are more excitable and hurried.

I keep walking and exploring. As I walk through downtown, a shoeshine worker stops me at almost every corner. They are always asking if I need a shine. I am wearing the cowboy boots I had when I arrived in Mexico. I look down at my boots and agree I could use a shine. The time I spend with the shoe-shine boys has an enormous influence on my learning Spanish. A good shine (limpiabotas) takes five to ten minutes. At first, my young shoe shiners correct my Spanish and laugh at me, but I find a way around them laughing. I offer them one tostone every time they correct my Spanish while shining my boots. That's about a nickel, very good money for them.

Hanging out in the streets turns out to be a good way to increase my vocabulary, but not great for my Spanish. People working in the streets have their own dialect, not a distinct language, just their own style and slang. Frequently, I tell a story at the dinner table, and am advised to find another word and not use street slang. Despite this drawback the people I meet on the street are more interesting in many ways than the people I live with. I find them easier to engage with, friendlier, and more accepting of me. Sure, I come from a family with money, education, and respect. But I have always seen myself as the troublemaker, an outsider whereas these people don't seem to care. They accept everyone they see on the street, so they accept me as well. Here, with ordinary people, I finally feel comfortable and at-home.

On the streets, with the workers, I feel the first stirring of interest in working with my hands, the beginning of my careers in construction and furniture making.

Chapter 3

Bush Mission with Uncle Bill

After six months in Jalapa, I'm feeling comfortable at Lucy's. I rarely see Margarita, Lupe, and Jose, who have their own routines with school and friends. While I am not socializing with the foreign students, I am discovering the town. My new family is constantly suggesting places to see and sharing of events happening in town. We have time together at home sharing stories, listening to music, and watching television. Tete and Tata, Lucy's aunts each have their own chair with cushioned seat cushions in the kitchen. They enjoy preparing meals and managing the outside help. Two other women come to the house most days for shopping, cleaning and laundry. Tata is more friendly. She learns my favorite foods and fits them into weekly meals. Lucy, a CPA and Catholic nun in an order of nuns who work and live outside a convent, goes to help families in the poorer neighborhoods every day. She brings my uncle with her regularly, and he helps with transportation, counseling, and running interference in domestic violence situations.

One day, at one of our regular lunch meetings, on the second floor of the market sitting at a metal table with a coca cola advertisement on top Uncle Bill tells me that Jesuit leaders are giving him orders to go on a bush mission in central and south Veracruz. The thrilling part is that he wants me to go with him! There are two reasons for the mission: first, to explore the educational, medical, political movements and protection of the people in the forested and jungle areas of Veracruz. The second, more fascinating reason is to explore the difficulty the existing missions are having with witchcraft in the area. When Uncle Bill tells my mother about the trip, the church ladies at Our Lady of Guadalupe Catholic Church in La Habra, California begin raising money for him. This a big deal for the ladies of the mission group, not only do they get to assist with the good work of the mission, but also to support my mom's beloved brother, Father Bill, the handsome, young, larger-than-life missionary priest.

Eventually the mission group raises enough money for Uncle Bill to purchase a used International Scout Jeep, the perfect vehicle for the trip through the jungle. Uncle Bill heads off to Mexico City to meet with the Jesuit council and returns with a list of the little towns and rural areas they want him visit. We pack up for the trip, collecting machetes, shovels, other tools for the jeep, a small generator, medical supplies, camping supplies and, everything we'll need to perform Mass on the road: a chalice, candles, vestments, communion hosts and wine. Uncle Bill, aka Padre Nolan, draws up an agenda, and writes letters to the mayors or heads of the communities we are to visit, letting them know we are on or way.

I know I will need a fresh supply of medication for

the trip, and Uncle Bill takes me to a nearby small pharmacy. To my amazement no prescription is needed, nothing. I just go to the counter to ask for the medicine, and they sell it to me, even this very specialized medicine.

This experience gets me thinking how I first started taking medication regularly. Our family pediatrician back home, Dr. McDonald, was tall, thin, funny with a personality we all loved and trusted. When he suggested to my mom that I visit a psychiatrist, Mom, in her positive, spirited manner, explained to me what to expect. I was around nine at the time, when the word psychiatrist inferred more than being a doctor. This more than freaked me out. Mom knew how this could be interpreted and agreed to keep it secret from my brothers and sister. This began a cycle of medication trials and trips to psychiatrists and psychologists. Even after several years of counseling, and testing, doctors could not come up with a diagnosis or explanation for my behaviors. The medications had terrible side effects. One medication left me almost paralyzed, crawling through the house and up and down stairs. For several days, while my body adjusted to it, I could not focus on anything. Sometimes I drooled, not able to control my mouth enough to talk or eat. My behavior was excellent, I was causing no trouble; but I was a zombie. Testing always came out the same, normal to high IQ. I should be a high achiever. What bothered me even more than the side effects was the sense that I was different and uncontrollable and had mental health problems. Some neighborhood families didn't want their kids hanging out with the "devil child."

Now in Veracruz I'm still taking pills, and I still hate how they make me sleepy, and interfere with my concentration and focus on important things like studying Spanish and feeling positive about myself.

Finally, we're ready and begin our journey, traveling on dirt roads that are barely roads at all, more like wide, muddy paths. We often need to dig the Scout out of the mud, removing large branches from the road and cutting brush away with our machetes. Even though the jungle terrain seems isolated and empty to me, somehow the local people know we are there and come out of nowhere to help us when we need it. Uncle Bill is working hard to learn to speak their unique dialect and getting good at it. I'm trying to learn all that I can, as well.

All these languages and dialects are difficult to learn because there are so many of them. Years later I took a further interest in these dialects and learned, Veracruz is the melting pot of Indian dialects and languages. Nahuatl is the most popular, followed by Totonaca and Huasteco. All are Aztec dialects, spoken on the coast and central areas, in these remote areas, people may not travel more than a five-mile radius of their home during their entire life; they developed dialects suited for the unique foods and environments in which they lived. For instance, in Cordoba, dwarfed by the mountain of Pico De Orizaba, we meet people on the south slope who have a word for oranges. On the north slope however they have apples, but no word for orange.

Uncle Bill and I share meals with the local people we stay with along the way. They help with directions and tell us about people we should meet. Everyday Padre Bill performs Mass on the hood of the Scout for excited crowds of people. Small groups from little towns of five to forty people gather, sometimes at a small hand-built church or a small plaza. The villagers dress in colorful native attire. The children are lively running around and playing. These are happy times.

We brought with us a Polaroid camera, and frisbees. Each is an enormous benefit in helping us introduce ourselves and bring small communities together. The Polaroid is magical. Having a picture develop in front of them is akin to sorcery. People stood with wide open eyes and suspicious looks on their faces. We take pictures of children playing with the frisbee, a toy they have never seen before. Uncle Bill has a couple dozen Frisbees and enough film for over a hundred pictures. This is a genius move on his part.

Saying Mass, taking pictures, sharing meals is great, but there are stall challenges to overcome. Some people are suspicious of our white skin, our different clothes, and boots. They wear huaraches (sandals), or go barefoot. We have a car; they have no cars. They would only see a truck once or twice a month, bringing supplies into their village. We have a generator at night for light. To build trust, despite our caution about eating some of the food we are served, we eat spider monkey and snake, obviously not our typical diet.

They serve us turkey, chicken, and pork as well. We are guests, so special foods are served, including bush meat. A popular dish is cornmeal and beans formed into a ball wrapped in a banana leaf and steamed, like a tamale. There are delicious but raised hell with my bowels.

The people we meet are simple - farmers, lumber cutters, and builders who all live off the land. They have no running water, no electricity, no supermarkets, no police, or firemen. Their lifestyle is communal. They all work together and help one another with their tasks and jobs. The inhabitants of these small villages stay in their own little villages, not venturing out into the wider world. Mirrors don't exist in this world. I have difficulty adjusting to looking into a piece of shiny metal, no bigger than three or four-inches square. Eventually I discover it is easier to see myself by looking into a still pond.

Several times a year, some villagers will go to a bigger town for a week or two where they sell vanilla and wild coffee they've collected. They also sell decorative fabrics made by the women, cloth that looks like needlepoint and tapestry combined and is woven on a back-strap loom. Backstrap looms, only 6 inches wide, are a traditional way to make narrow strips of cloth used for belts, scarves and colorful accents on dresses and clothing. These specialized, beautiful, handcrafted wares are worth a lot in the marketplace.

Even though the profits from selling theses goods are welcomed by the villagers they often encounter prejudice in the larger towns, the experience is not always positive. The Indian cultures are not popular with Mexicans, even though Mexicans are part Indian and part Spanish. I am told that the reason Mexican men wear mustaches and women do not shave their legs and underarms is to show they are more Spanish than Indian, as Indians have little body hair. In Southern Mexico Indians are not allowed to attend school with Mexican children, or work in any Mexican-owned establishments. They can only provide services. This prejudice affects us as well, and on some occasions when local Mexicans treat Uncle Bill and me with distrust, we realize that our close connection to the tribal Indians is responsible.

As we travel south in the steamy and misty forests, we come to the village of Zongolica, a small farm community. Uncle Bill lets me know we are stopping there because of the witchcraft in this area. These black magic practices have been interfering with the churches and keeping people away, due to their fear of angering the practitioners of black magic. Our task is to get a better understanding of the dynamic between the brujos (witches) and the Catholic church. We head to Lake Catemaco, the capital of witchcraft in Mexico, population 27,000 people. In the areas surrounding Zongolica and Lake Catemaco, when brujos enter small village churches during Mass, the entire congregation flees in fear. Brujos isolate themselves from the ordinary villagers, in their own enclaves and in nearby caves.

We head out to the villages of Santiago, Tuxtla, Comoapan, Palenque, Santa Maria, and Jaltipan. In 1968, these are very remote areas with isolated populations. The inditos, or Indians of the forest, have superstitious beliefs that date back thousands of years to when the Aztecs were engaged in human sacrifice. Brujos instill fear in the people with their animal sacrifices, satanic cleansing dances and taking of hallucinogenic herbs. The altars they build in their homes and the surrounding caves are scary, with burnt bones, blood, and pieces of clothing from the dead.

The Catholic church has been battling witchcraft since the discovery of the Americas in the 1500s. What I learned while trying to educate myself on brujos and witchcraft in Mexico is what a complex subject this is. Witchcraft in Mexico includes the concept of the Christian devil brought from Spain by Franciscan friars during the insurrection, Caribbean religions derived from Africa and various other African beliefs and rituals brought to Mexico on slave ships.

Uncle Bill had gifts for the leaders of these small villages, which helps to break down barriers and makes it easier to talk with them. The superstitions separating the Church and witchcraft will not go away easily. Uncle Bill and I talk many times about whether we are bringing the right or wrong message by siding with the church. These people are living in paradise, with beautiful lakes and mountains, no worries, and an abundance of food. Maybe the ethical thing is to leave them alone to their own ways. The brujos are not hurting anyone, they only scare people. We meet with an anthropological team of three, from France before we leave. They are there to approximate a timeline of how long it might take the Indians in this area of Veracruz to catch up to modern civilization and technology. They have not finished their study, yet predict it will be around five hundred years. I am astonished to be surrounded by people living five hundred years behind me.

After completing our work in Zongolica, we have some extra time in our schedule, and travel around in our muddy Scout. We pass numerous people offering to clean the car. We pass a man with his son, a ladder, a hose and a smile and they get the job. Uncle Bill is interested that anthropologists have found only twenty-five percent of the anthropological sites in the area. We drive to Palenque, a Mayan ruin, still mostly unexplored. With our machetes in hand and with local help, we cut through the forest and brush to see structures surrounding a central pyramid. The process of uncovering and cleaning these ancient sites is slow, understandable after seeing the centuries of mold, moss, and vegetation they are moldering under. Today, in 2023, the land surrounding Palenque is clean, with all the overgrowth of the jungle removed. But when we are there, it is difficult to visualize how it will look with everything uncovered. The local people entertain us, showing us artifacts and telling stories of the area. After we pull out the Polaroid and take a few pictures of the people, they offer us gifts of small flat stones with carved symbols on them. The Mayans used hieroglyphic stamps to write with. I find these more interesting than the burnt bones and blood of the Brujos.

Heading back to Jalapa, we take the long route along the coast and enjoy the towns and food along the way. The seafood is delicious. I'll never forget the small fishing village of Lizardo at the mouth of a river on the coast, where the shrimp are the size of hotdogs. Before leaving the coast, we stay a day and night at La Playa de Chachalacas, a little north of Veracruz, along the Gulf of Mexico. Miles of sandy beaches and places to eat. Hotels have no air conditioning, so we rent two hammocks on the beach and spend the night. It feels like heaven.

Chapter 4

New Friends – Back in Jalapa

Uncle Bill and I were gone from Jalapa for three months. When we returned, things had changed. The students I had been spending time with were gone, and I was once again alone. Wanting to meet new friends, I began hanging out with a group I did not need. A group of young guys my age east of downtown. They were not going to school, or working, just cruising the neighborhood. I could see myself slipping downward in this direction all the way back to junior high school.

In our upper middle-class family, I was exposed to the best, but I drifted to the worst. The kids I hung out with were frequently in school detention or sitting in the principal's office. I am not a good student. I am failing my classes. The medication I am taking makes it impossible to focus on any of my classes. I've been labeled as a failing student. My only friends were labeled the same. By the time I was thirteen we'd started smoking, drinking, and experimenting with recreational drugs. Mom and dad were going crazy, unable to fix or even understand the problem. I know

now how difficult it must have been for them, raising five children with me taking all the fun, laughter, and time away from the others. Eventually they had had enough. The family was becoming disruptive, fearful, confused, and anxious. My siblings quit inviting their friends over because they feared my disruptions.

I had a great-uncle who became famous during WWII. Father William Nolan, my mother's uncle, a chaplain in the Navy, became famous for saying during the Pearl Harbor attack "Praise the Lord and pass the ammunition" and for that made the front cover of Life magazine. My parents thought that enrolling me in a military school run by Dominican Catholic nuns would be my salvation and the answer to all their prayers. Yes, boot camp was the answer, and the best part is the school would have to accept me, since. I was the great-nephew of Father William Nolan, in whose honor they had dedicated Saint Catherine's Military Boarding School in Anaheim, California.

All though elementary school I was taught by Catholic nuns of the order of Sisters of Saint Joseph, a kind order of teaching nuns. The Dominican nuns had a different reputation, they are tough disciplinarians, nuns who rapped fingers with a wooden pointer. Would they punish me for behaviors I had no control over? I hoped someone would diagnose my problem soon so I wouldn't have to go to Saint Catherine's. Mom and Dad had long discussions with the school about me, my mental health, and the school's expectations. Everyone agreed, my parents, their friends, my doctors, and teachers, that a good kick in the ass by a bunch of Dominican Nuns would fix whatever was wrong with me. I would begin the summer school program after seventh grade. If school went well, I would continue at Saint Catherine's for eighth grade in the fall. The separation from my siblings and parents in a military boarding school sounded unthinkable and painful, and I felt abandoned.

Before I left for school, a new symptom appeared. When arguing with my father one time, I stopped dead in my tracks, staring into space, the right side of my face trembling. He shouted, "Get that look off of your face."

I could not hear him, nor did I know my face was quivering. After a few moments I snapped out of it, and my father sent me to my room for disobeying him. No one knew I was having an epileptic seizure. My father concluded I was purposely disrespecting him. No one imagined that seizures might be a part of my problem.

My father constantly pushed me to be behave better. My behavior was out of control. I would get so confused, anxious and frustrated I would break anything in sight, cussing and cursing my father using every four letter I knew. Going to Saint Catherine's military school for the summer became a threat. I felt devastated and powerless. Not knowing where to turn. I would go to my room and cry. I turned to prayer, praying for some crazy intervention that would rescue me from the potential fury of the nuns. A few days later, following another seizure, my father slapped me, trying to wipe that look off my face. I didn't even realize he'd slapped me until mom brought me a tissue to stop my bleeding lip. Within a week, I was off to military school.

Saint Catherine was what I expected. They awakened us early, and we were ordered to march in single file to the cafeteria, then to class and to daily Mass. In the afternoons, we went to our dorm and took showers with the nuns watching over our adolescent nakedness. I continued to do something wrong daily. Leaving my desk without asking, talking back, not staying in line when marching. In response the nun liked to twist my ear until bright red or smack me with a two-foot-long paddle. One day they caught me stuffing the carrot-raisin salad, which I hated, into my empty half-pint milk carton and throwing it away. My punishment was to fish though the trash, open every milk carton and eat any food stuffed inside. When I refused, I got another paddling.

Two weeks later, I sat outside Mother Superior's office in the middle of the day, waiting for my parents to arrive. I did not know why I was there. When they arrived, we went into Mother Superior's office and were told I was being expelled from school and must leave by the end of the day. My parents were devastated, but they had no choice but to load me and my things into the car and drive home. Later, my mother explained to me what had happened. Early that morning someone knocked over a statue of the Virgin Mary. Afterward, each of us, about thirty boys, had to come forward, pick up the statue, kiss it and say a prayer. I must have had a seizure when they handed me the statue. The nuns described how my face started trembling and instead of kissing the statue I dropped the Virgin Mary to the ground, where she broke into pieces. They accused me of throwing the statue to the ground. When we got home, my father asked me, "What are we going to do now?"

I must have said something like, "I don't know or care," and after that all hell broke loose.

I can still picture the red finger marks on my mother's face from where my father slapped her. Back in my bedroom, I sat and thought about what had just happened, believing it was all my fault, the years of being the child who caused them terrible disappointment. Upstairs my mom was crying and putting makeup on the hand marks my father's hand had left on the side of her face. I acted like I did not see the bruising beginning to form and apologized to her for causing so many problems. Seeing my mother take the blame for my actions felt unbearable. All the next week, Mom did not go out while the red finger marks faded. Dad seemed to work late a lot that week, arriving home just in time for dinner. Mark, Gary, Luke and Annie knew something had happened but just watched with enormous eyes, knowing not to talk about it.

I knew I was to blame - for my undiagnosed seizures, my behavior, my failure to admit that I made my face quiver and failed to respond to my father's demand to stop. Yet at the same time, I never understood what he was accusing me of. I didn't know. I didn't know. I didn't know. I cried, yelled, ran, swore, destroyed property, and pleaded with my dad to believe me, but he did not.

All summer, I stayed home, waiting for my freshman year in high school to begin. Weekly appointments with psychiatrists, psychologists, new medicine trials and visits from some of my dad's friends, who would drop by to give me pep talks. Mr. Lavin came by, and like a TV cop, said, "Let's talk outside."

Standing in the driveway, he would offer me a cigarette and try to delve into my mind. I was always polite while I waited for the conversation to end, knowing he was wasting both of our time.

Once again, my parents enrolled me in a Catholic school, St. Paul's, High School, known for its disciplined structure. To this day, I cannot figure out why the school accepted me. It may have been my parents' ability to pay the expensive tuition. In this school, like the others, I didn't last long. Only a month later my teacher, a Catholic Brother, dragged me out of a classroom by my ear. Sitting in the principal's office waiting for my parents to pick me up, I was told that I had stood up in class and started wandering around, being disrespectful and insubordinate, not obeying the teacher's direction to sit down.

Waiting there for two hours for my mom and dad, I knew what to expect. My mom would be sympathetic and protective. My father would express a low level of disgust. I say "low level" because I believe that deep down, my father loved me and wanted to help. Still, I would be held responsible for what happened. When my parents arrived, it only took a few minutes. My parents were told, I was not a good fit for Saint Paul's, and should seek another school that would better suit my needs. As near as I could tell, my only need was for someone to accept me as the good person and not expect me to change when I had no control over what was happening to me.

Out of school again, back home, taking meds, seeing a psychiatrist and psychologists every two weeks. My friends had not changed. I was still hanging out with the wrong kids.

My new friends in Jalapa smoked pot, listened to music, and sat around talking. They were all neighbors, two brothers and two other guys. One brother, Jorge, had a handicap, apparently polio. The family lived in a nice, upper-class neighborhood and had several women working in the home. One was an attendant for Jorge. She helped him around and made sure the path he was walking on was clear and that he didn't trip. Because he could not stand normally at the toilet and urinate; he peed in a bucket, and she emptied it. We all sat together while I translated American war resistance music from English into Spanish. The marijuana was excellent. Our drug connection was a man we called Coconut. To get pot, we'd sit high on a loam next to the train track where the trains stopped. If Coconut jumped off the train with a coconut in one hand, we knew he had pot. If no coconut, no pot. A simple system that worked well for us.

To expand my experience in Mexico, my friends planned a trip to Mexico City to show me around. They knew the city and had friends where we could stay. We rode a bus to Mexico City, arriving in the afternoon, settled in, had a meal, and got high on pot. In the morning, we headed off to one of the city's large open markets, the Sonoran market, tailored to people from the Northern Sonora Desert.

At the market, the only item my friends were interested in was peyote, the hallucinogenic cactus. Though illegal in the U.S., you could buy it by the gunnysack at the market. Jorge decided to buy a liter of peyote juice rather than a gunny sack of cactus buttons. We asked for a liter and watched in amazement as they used a juice press to convert several kilos of peyote buttons into a glass liter bottle. When they were done, we went to the second floor of the market, where food was prepared. At the juice and milkshake kiosk, we asked for strawberry shakes with a shot of our peyote in each glass. Peyote can make you throw up because of the taste if you are not careful so we mixed it with fruit juice to help keep it down. A one-ounce shot is about three or four buttons. We were all stoned, I mean stoned, spending the rest of the day wandering around the different markets and shops in the city. We stayed one more night and then returned to Jalapa.

I continued to hang out with these guys, even though I knew it was a mistake. Still trying to work on my Spanish and learn about the culture of Jalapa, I vowed not to let my new learning experience run parallel to my past experiences.

After St. Paul's my parents had run out of private school options and I started at the public high school, Sonora High. I was a magnet for the students getting in trouble, skipping school, smoking, going over to friends' houses in the middle of the day to smoke pot. One friend, Tom Coffey, a neighbor, and I walked to school together every day. Tom's dad was a doctor and his mother a nurse. Tom smoked pot and drank, but he seemed different from my other friends. He had a quality I later understood as compassion. Tom knew I had problems. He had heard the commotion coming from our house. I went over to his home almost every school morning, just to get out of my house and escape dad who would quiz me all morning about school and what was going on, offering what seemed like an endless lecture on how to make myself better and how I should act. I was jealous of Tom. Usually, he'd be sitting down for breakfast when I came over. I'd sit in the den and watch television while his family sat together in the kitchen. I noticed they always set the table for breakfast. Milk and juice on the table, with an assortment of dry cereals to select from, and two or three vitamins in each cereal bowl. Mornings in my house were different. Mom had started drinking more and rarely woke up to get us off to school. When my father wasn't lecturing me, he ate by himself in the dining room, reading the newspaper while my brothers and sister and I had to fend for ourselves. Most days, our breakfast involved finding a box of cereal or drinking a glass of Carnation Instant Breakfast. Daily vitamins were not to be found. It was hit-or-miss on whether we might see Mom before we left for school.

Tom had two older brothers, Terry, and Tim, who were troublemakers. They began offering Tom and me drugs. These included Seconal, a downer, and speed, or crank. We accepted the drugs and often took them before school, which was a disaster. I found myself again in the principal's office for multiple school offenses. The worst was when I had seizures at school. During a seizure, I was incoherent and didn't hear or feel anything. The word got out, and the bullies moved in. One day, I was standing in the hall next to my locker between classes when a few boys saw me gazing off in a seizure and started roughing me up and pushing me around. I came out of the seizure and found myself on the floor, my books and papers scattered everywhere. Students hovered over me, laughing like kids do. I felt shame and embarrassment. My math teacher, Mr. Lukas, helped me up, ushered me to the principal's office. They were concerned and asked all kinds of questions. Who knocked you down? What happened out there? Are you hurt? I had not yet been diagnosed with a seizure disorder and had no explanation of what happened.

Walking home from school talking to Thom, I revealed to him that sometimes I lost awareness of time and space and, when it was over, I'd find myself somewhere else. I didn't know where the time went or what had happened. Tom said he'd watch out for me.

It was only the first week at school, and already my seizures were in the open, I'd been beat up, sent to the principal's office, accused of fighting, and hadn't finished any homework. That night, like so many others, I lay in bed thinking, what am I going to do? What's happening to me? Is there any way out of this?

Day after day at school, the same boys followed me around, waiting for me to seize so they could watch the freak wandering around with his face quivering. Tom was always there when I came out of it, helping me up and back to my next class. I was always sleepy and tired after my episodes. Teachers became concerned that I was sleeping in their classes and falling behind. Defending myself, all I could say was that I didn't know what was going on.

One day, during Mr. Lukas' math class. I stood up and walked around the classroom, then walked out of the room, not responding to anything Mr. Lukas was saying. He followed me out and directed me to the nurse's office. When I came to, the nurse and principal were there, said they wanted to help me and meet with my parents. I felt listened to. Believing they wanted to help, I hoped this may be the turning point.

The day of the meeting, the principal, the school nurse, Mr. Lukas, and my mom, dad and I met. The principal had reviewed my records and knew my school history at St. Paul's and St. Catherine's. They talked a lot about my safety when I was experiencing these episodes. Mr. Lukas seemed to have a little knowledge of what might be happening. He asked my parents if doctors had ever considered these episodes to be Petit mal seizures, which are common in childhood epilepsy. I could tell my parents didn't want to go there. Epilepsy in the 1960s was a mysterious topic and viewed as a scary mental disease, that people did not openly discuss. The principal and nurse said they would monitor me, but I would have to show some progress in my schoolwork. We all agreed and left. Progressing in school is difficult when seizing, taking medication, and sleeping. To me, the writing was on the wall. This school would not work out either.

I started to self-medicate. Though I knew that recreational drugs were not a medicine to cure epilepsy. I was grasping for anything to help relieve the mental pain. I felt like a freak and a failure, with a weird mental disorder. Tom was a friend, and also a good drug connection. He had keys to his father's medical office. I felt safe doing drugs in a doctor's office. Both of us shot up prescription drugs like uppers, downers, and pain meds. Thinking we knew what we were doing, we read the pharmaceutical books in the office on which drugs were safest and best. We even weighed ourselves, so we would use the correct dosage.

Our self- prescribed drug use came to a halt one day when we had the not so brilliant idea to shoot up whiskey. Tom tried it first, just a small amount, yet he fell to the ground. Emergency 911 did not yet exist, so we were on our own. I grabbed a washcloth, soaked it in cold water, splashed it on Tom's face and yelled at him to wake up. I slapped him over and over to rouse him. A minute, or should I say a lifetime later, Tom woke up, a little unsteady but happy to be alive. This scared the shit out of both of us and we never went back to his father's office again. LSD was becoming popular in the middle sixties, and we reasoned that if George Harrison and John Lennon took it, so could we. Tom and I both got a little piece of paper with LSD on it from his brother Terry, who gave us strict instructions to be in a quiet place, find a safe area with an exit or in an open field. LSD was a mind-bending exaggeration of all five senses. A pleasant trip, no coughing, no strong odors, and no paraphernalia to carry around. Tom and I agreed to take another hit of

LSD before school one morning. After that for the next three months of school, I cut classes forty-three days, taking drugs, drinking, and partying. Unbeknownst to me, the school called home every day to see where I was, my mom covered for me every time.

My office visits to the psychiatrist never stopped. My current psychiatrist was in a wheelchair, an empathetic and friendly man who was easy to talk to. During one of our sessions, the doctor went out to the waiting room, telling my mom, "I just saw John have a seizure. I saw it firsthand, and I think I know what we are dealing with." I've never forgotten the look on my mom's face, her expression filled with hope. Mom cried, and so did I. The doctor said he wanted to consult with a colleague, and we'd meet again soon.

That night, after mom explained everything to my dad, I saw my father cry for the first time, in happiness. Mom, being the rational person in the home, reminded us that this was only a start. She was so excited she gathered my siblings together to announce things were going to change and their big brother was going to get better.

Several days later, the psychiatrist called to schedule a visit. The three of us, me, mom, and dad, met at his office. The doctor explained that the type of seizure I had was the first one he had ever seen. After reviewing my case with his associates, he believed he had witnessed a right frontal lobe seizure or psychomotor seizure. Little information about this type of seizure existed, but many studies were being conducted on seizures originating from the right temporal lobe. I liked this doctor. He was younger, in his thirties. He didn't wear a white doctors coat, just a sport shirt and jeans. He talked to me more like a friend, having his own problems being in a wheelchair he showed real compassion. A medication for this type of seizure had shown some success. I wanted to try it, but the doctor cautioned me. Starting this medication would require me to be hospitalized for two days to monitor how my body reacted. We agreed to all the protocols. Drug trials would begin the following week.

I sat down with my parents that night and we talked about school. I told them I wanted to drop out. We all had preconceived ideas that only stupid kids, or bad kids, quit high school but I wanted to leave for medical reasons. Even this concept was hard to accept. Dropping out of school felt humiliating to me. Families like ours didn't have high school dropouts. Both my mother and father had gone to college. My siblings will all be going to private Catholic high schools. My parents' friends would not dream of their children dropping out of school. Even so, we agreed we would do whatever it took for me to get better. The next morning, Mom called the school to explain the situation and I was unenrolled from Sonora High School.

The next week, I entered the hospital and started the medication. I was happy to be there, even though on the first day my legs wobbled, and I could stand only with support. My mind was fuzzy, I had no appetite, and I was slurring my words. The second day was a little better and on the third day I left with a prescription for Mysoline, an anticonvulsant with many side effects. The three most profound side effects I experienced were hyperactivity, restlessness, and confusion. None of that mattered to me. I was ready to control my seizures and start living.

This solution was not perfect. I still had seizures although they were more infrequent and shorter. The best part was having a name for what was wrong and being able to explain to people what was happening. I lost friends when the word of my epilepsy diagnosis surfaced. There was still a terrible stigma attached to epilepsy, even though it was not considered a major mental illness like schizophrenia, bipolar, severe OCD, or depression. Today I know how those with mental illness feel, being stigmatized for an illness that is not your fault. The pain is a deep anguishing sense of guilt and rejection.

Mom continued drinking too much. This stigma that hung over me, also hung-over mom, and dad. Having a son with epilepsy carried its own shame. An ill son and being Irish was a perfect excuse to drink. Mons's drinking did not start with my illness. Dad was a successful salesman. In the 1950's being a salesman included the three-martini lunch, and endless entertainment with customers at nice restaurants with your wife. All of this contributed to her drinking as well. Mom carried other demons with her as excuses for drinking. The death of her older brother in World War Two, her mother committing suicide at age thirty-six and a host of other reasons factored into her alcoholism. Mom was not a sloppy drunk, she was a social drunk, not always appearing drunk but always under the influence. She was greatly loved by all my brothers and sister's friends. They trusted my mom and came to our house frequently to discuss problems they were having with her.

I hung out in the house all day, every day, for weeks while she tried to live her life, explaining to her friends what was wrong with me, and her fears about what the outcome would be. I think my father's fear was mainly how their social life would be affected. Mental illness was not a popular conversation piece.

A therapist once named the feelings my parents were experiencing as Gray Death, a condition where you recognize that the son or daughter you brought into the world is gone. The child who you planned on doing well in school, healthy, and playing sports, going to the school prom, entering college, and getting married, has died. You now have a new child who you must love for who they are. Conversations with friends are difficult and complicated: friends' distance themselves. Invitations for parties and dinners stop arriving, they find conversations about a child with epilepsy to difficult.

After a year in Jalapa, now seventeen years old, I don't want to get caught again in the bad behavior I'd experienced before coming to Mexico. I'm here to learn and to be the best I can be, even with having seizures. I wondered frequently whether I was achieving my goals. Lucy and I were getting along, although I'm sure she had received word of who my new friends were. I was determined to try to focus and find new activities. Uncle Bill was busy doing what priests do, but we spent more time together. We often went to the beach in Chachalaca or took day trips to swim in a lake. I became more interested in all the cultural and anthropological sites and history of Veracruz and southern Mexico.

I started visiting the Museum of Anthropology in Jalapa. The Olmec culture was the highlight of the museum. Predating the Mayan, Aztec and Inca civilization, Olmec culture was discovered in the state of Veracruz. in Texistepec. The Olmec civilization dated back to the Pre-Classical Mesoamerica period of 1200 BC. They practiced human sacrifice and believed in demons and ancient witchcraft. I was fascinated to learn that the brujos I had just visited with Uncle Bill in Tuxtla and Catemato were descendants of the Olmec culture. It turned out that Uncle Bill knew someone at the museum, and I got a small job sorting pamphlets, brochures, and books in a back room. I made little money but was proud to make constructive use of my time. My parents were thrilled, and my dad even started sending me a little more money each month.

Life was good. I had a place to live, a job, three meals a day, and an interest in something. Whenever I could, I took trips to cultural and anthropological sites. There were so many to explore. I took a trip to Texistepec, to see the giant sculptures of the Olmec heads and pyramids. I visited Mexico City alone and spent time at Chapultepec Park, the largest park in Latin America, which is twice the size of New York's Central Park. The museums were exceptional, and I spent a lot of time there. Seeing the city this way, calm and relaxed compared to when I first arrived, experiencing the riots and shootings during the Olympics, or being high on peyote with my friends.

I stayed in a different section of Mexico City than I'd stayed before. I rented a small room in a hotel in Zona Rosa. A shared bathroom was at the end of a long corridor and my room had one window that looked out to an alley behind a small cantina or bar. My second-floor room was small, and had little ventilation. Walls in the room must have had the original paint, maybe twenty years old. The one redeeming feature of the hotel was its safe location in an affordable part of the city.

After getting settled into my room I went out to visit the bar behind the hotel for a beer. With my white skin and long red hair the men at the bar had something to look at. They were all much older than me and started joking around, asking me about the pretty women in California. It was getting dark when I left, found something to eat, and returned to my room. Several hours later, I heard a knock at the door. I answered, and a very inebriated man from the bar pointed to his nose and asked, "Como se dice in English?" I said "nose" and closed the door. The same thing happened two more times that night: drunken men knocking at my door, laughing, and asking me stupid questions.

Later that night, drunken men sitting outside the now closed bar in the alley awakened me, sitting below my window, singing. I yelled at them to stop. The singing stopped for a few minutes and started back up. I needed some sleep and went down to the manager's room to complain. The man at the front desk reached into a drawer and handed me a gun, a small BB gun and said, "Shoot them and they will stop". I went back to my room, opened the window, and waited for them to start singing again. When the singing began, I stuck the BB gun out the window, shot and hit one man on the arm. He reached up and swatted his arm, yelling "Mosca! Mosca! (mosquito, mosquito)". I shot five or six more times, hitting the men. All the men were yelling "Mosca! Mosca!" and they eventually wandered off. The next morning, I returned the gun, thanking the man at the front desk, and said it worked great. He responded, "It always does."

Back in Jalapa, I met up with Uncle Bill who reminded me we had missed celebrating my seventeenth birthday. Bill thought since I was seventeen, I should get a driver's license and a better ID. I also needed to upgrade my visa; it had expired several months earlier. This meant another trip to Mexico City, to the American Embassy. I knew how to drive; I had driven often on our trip through Veracruz. The Embassy had nothing to do with driver's licenses. We had to go across town to the State licensing office. Getting a license was pretty informal with two old wooden desks in a room. There were ten to fifteen people in front of us, everyone waiting on the sidewalk. Street vendors, beggars, shoeshine boys and insurance salesman all had a captive audience standing in line. All we needed was for someone to vouch that I could drive and pay for the license. A few hundred pesos, and that was all it took. I didn't have to show proof of insurance, take a skills test, eye test, or anything. When we left, Uncle Bill had me drive out of town. The traffic in Mexico

City was impossible. Buses, cars, bikes, and scooters everywhere. We came up to a roundabout, or Reforma, an intersection with about ten streets coming together congested with cars, everyone's hand on the horn. You had to be quick, fast, and brave to maneuver going around the Reforma. I pulled it off, and we made it through by the skin of our teeth with no accident.

We spent the night in a hotel and had an excellent dinner at a pleasant restaurant. I learned two lessons on this trip. One was to always leave a little trash on the floor of the hotel room. There was no full-time housekeeping or cleaning staff. So, if the room was a little dirty, the manager ran out to the street and paid someone a few pesos to clean it up. The second lesson was to keep a bottle of warm gin under your car seat when driving in Mexico City, to settle your nerves in traffic.

On our drive back, we stopped in Puebla. Uncle Bill wanted to show me a few more sites and give me a little more history. As we drove back to Jalapa, Bill shared with me his role as a priest there. An Olympic swimming and boxing coach for the 1964 Olympics and a prison chaplain, he was now working in poor neighborhoods, finding families that needed help, teaching boxing and working out with kids. He served Mass almost every day for the Indians that spoke Nahuatl, a Mayan dialect he had studied and learned. He heard confessions and worked with the Indian populations that did not speak Spanish, helping them with social issues and personal problems. Uncle Bill was a Catholic priest but not always on the side of the church or "Canon Law". He explained to me what the church was like when Mexico was conquered by the Spaniards in the 1500s. The church instilled fear in the people and it still exists. Bill told me women would confess to him they had made love to their husbands for pleasure and not to have children. He would try to explain that this was not a sin. He was not against women taking birth control after they had, six or seven children and were living in poverty. Bill was a common-sense man and told it as he saw it. Uncle Bill shared with me that he was having issues with his superiors, and was being watched by the local diocese for preaching ideas the church did not support. Everyone in town liked Padre Nolan. The church just didn't know what to do with him.

One day, at lunch, he informed me that he received orders to leave Mexico and go to Brazil. I felt devastated. In Mexico with Bill, I found a new life free from my past. Bill would not be leaving for a few months, but when he left, I could no longer live at Lucy's. I had to figure something out soon.

Chapter 5

A Visit Home

Jalapa has been my home for the last two years. Soon, Uncle Bill will leave for Brazil; it is time for me to decide whether to return home to California or stay in Mexico on my own without Uncle Bill's support. I already know what my decision will be. My life in Mexico is new, exciting, and free from the stigma of epilepsy. Uncle Bill, aware of how much I enjoy living in Mexico and how well I am doing, invites me to the church rectory to talk. Our conversation is not pastoral but feels fatherlier. Lucy no longer wants me to live in her home after he leaves for Brazil. This is not what either of us wants to hear, but Uncle Bill has an idea.

He has already contacted a friend, the mayor of Sitala, a village in the Chiapas highlands, to let him know his nephew may be visiting. Uncle Bill tells me of his experience as a Jesuit priest in Sitala for several years, learning the Tzeltal language and living within their unique culture. He is creating an opportunity for me that no one else can, and he wants me to take it. I wholeheartedly agree. With this idea in my mind, I plan a call home to say I want to come back to visit. It is important for me to see my family and reconnect with them. But I have several questions. Do they expect me to come home and stay? Am I welcome to come visit and then head back to Mexico? Will they still give me some financial support? I am unsure what they will say, but I want to share my life and experiences in Jalapa with them. I'm seventeen, with no high school diploma, no job skills, and only my parent's home to return to. I have no clue about what lies ahead. I know my parents care for and love me, yet I also know that if I live at home, it will be under their conditions, not mine. I need to find out fast if there is anything for me in California.

With these uncertainties lingering in my mind, I make a plan to leave Jalapa in a week. I tell everyone here that this is only a visit to California. I will return in a few weeks. The trip home is a fifty-dollar, three-day bus ride to the border. Wanting to spend as little money as possible, I decide to hitchhike as far as Guadalajara. The area between Jalapa and Guadalajara is well populated, so traveling should not be a problem, although crossing the northern Sonoran Desert could be dangerous if I get stuck without water or shelter in the sweltering heat. From Guadalajara I will take a bus to Tijuana. San Diego is just across the border.

Hitchhiking to Guadalajara turns out to be quick and uneventful, me sitting in the backseat of someone else's car minding my own business. The bus ride to Tijuana is crowded and boring. I sit next to a woman who must weigh four hundred pounds and snores. Being friendly, I offer her a stick of chewing gum, then tuck the pack in the pocket in front of my seat and take a nap. When I awaken an hour later and reach for the gum, the package is empty. She is chewing away on the entire pack. For the rest of the day, we have no interactions.

Arriving in Tijuana, I call home. I eat some food and wait for my parents' arrival. Two hours later, we have a grand reunion with hugs and kisses all around. Mom insists we wait until we get home before we talk. Back home, we have lunch and talk for hours. Predictably, Mom thinks I'm too thin and that she needs to fatten me up. We discuss my health, and I let them know I am still having seizures, but they are less of a problem, that people in Jalapa accept me for who I am, including my seizures.

My brothers and sister, eagerly jump into the conversation. Each of them Mark, Gary, Luke, and Ann look different and older. I keep commenting on their new clothing and their long and shaggy Beatle hair styles. After speaking Spanish and learning different Indian dialects for so long I have begun to forget words in English, which they find hilarious. They keep teasing me, which helps to break the ice between us.

Later, I see a few old friends and receive the bad news that two of my friends died in the Vietnam War. Such a loss. They were only eighteen years old. The worst news is that a good friend came back from the war addicted to heroin and later died of an overdose. It hits me hard, not knowing what to think or how to react to losing friends at such a young age due to drug addiction and a war no one wanted.

Once home, I can see that life has been easier for everyone in my absence. My brothers and sister are in private schools, playing sports and able to have friends over to the house. The family goes on vacations without worrying about me acting out. No doctor appointments, no drug trials and no constant observation, looking for additional side effects of the medicines. My parents have more time to themselves. They will not admit it, but I can see the family is happier.

We talk about the idea Uncle Bill proposed about traveling to Sitala. He has already planned for me to visit and maybe stay longer. I clearly explain that this is what I want to do, and they can see my determination. After we discuss my plans, they agree to continue to support me returning to Mexico.

Before I leave, I have an opportunity to paint a neighbor's house and make some money. Dad seems unsettled by my staying longer, perhaps because he can see I have matured and become more confident. I am more independent and more self-reliant and am accustomed to making my own decisions. He knows I no longer have the behavior problems I once had and that he had to manage. One day when I am painting, he walks by the house, looks up at me on the roof and says, "You are no longer a son of mine."

This comment hurt me deeply; those words are the worst I have ever heard. What have I done? There are no behavior problems now and I'm doing my best not to be in the way. Has he abandoned me?

Looking back, I realize my past problems were more than my father could handle. He never educated himself about my seizure disorder, instead depending on Mom, who took responsibility for my health and mental well-being. Perhaps my father's work, providing for the family and his lack of knowledge of my condition, caused him to distance himself. It got to a point that I no longer felt he was my dad. He didn't want to deal with my problems anymore. He felt the stigma and was ashamed his son had epilepsy. There was nothing else I could do but let him know I loved him.

When the paint job is complete, I prepare to leave. I spend my last week with my brothers and sister and talking to mom. I never tell mom what dad said to me at our neighbor's house. That would be too painful for her. My mother's love and care are enough for me. Time is up for me in California, and I'm ready to get back to Mexico.

Part Two

Map

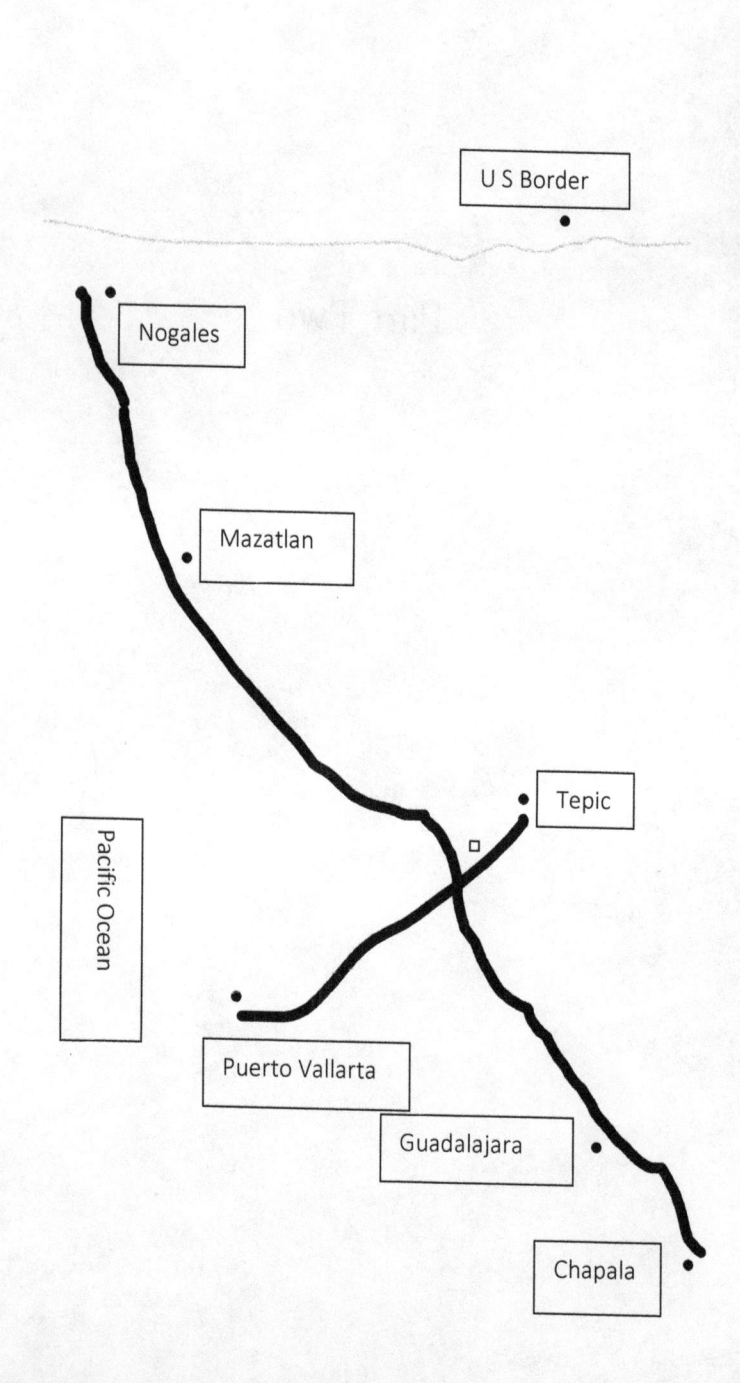

- U S Border
- Nogales
- Mazatlan
- Tepic
- Pacific Ocean
- Puerto Vallarta
- Guadalajara
- Chapala

Chapter 6

Heading Back Through Nogales

In the summer of 1970, leaving home again, I take the bus from Los Angeles to Nogales, Texas, where I board a train to Mexico City. Waiting at the station, I meet several American students returning to the University of Mexico City to start classes. We talk about how the train may be crowded and the air-conditioning not working, making the trip uncomfortable. We come up with an idea: to ride on top of the train while crossing the desert. While the train is boarding, we climb the ladder with our water, snacks, and rope. The conductor scowls and watches us but says nothing. We feel the wind on our face, as we pass the Chihuahua mountains rising out of the desert with a clear blue sky above. I see roadrunners, quail, and mountain goats roaming. Riding on top of the train is much better than being below sitting on a hot and sticky vinyl seat.

At first, I don't think about what could happen if I have a seizure if I were to get up and walk off the edge of the train roof. Of course, there is a chance, but my mind has never let me hurt myself during a seizure. With the power of youthful thinking, I feel sure everything will be fine.

The snacks and water do not last long. We stop a few times during the day for pickups and drop- offs. At each stop, we have time to climb down to grab food from the vendors waiting on the platform. At one layover, the conductor gets our attention and explains to us that in a few hours, we will come to a long tunnel. He says, "The clearance between the top of the tunnel and the train is only one foot. If you are on top of the train, you will become shredded cabbage" and laughs. We give up and come down, to prevent us from becoming coleslaw.

For the next two days, we follow this daily pattern, riding the top of the train during the day and finding a seat below at night until we reach the port town of Mazatlán. From there, I take a side trip to the coastal town of Puerto Vallarta. Summer is boiling hot in Puerto Vallarta. After walking the boardwalk, sampling food and visiting the central market, I find the bus station and buy a ticket to Mexico City.

The bus does not leave until that evening, so I wander the boardwalk in the afternoon trying to find a place to stay cool. Close to the bus station, I stop at a cantina for a cold soda. The bar is full. I drop my backpack next to the door and grab a seat. Only five minutes have passed before a police car drives up, a policeman jumps out and grabs my backpack, then drives off. Another policeman comes into the bar and asks, whose bag was at the door? The bartender points to me. The police said they saw me drinking on the sidewalk and to come with them to retrieve my backpack. What else could I do? Arguing with them was useless. Speaking Spanish was my only advantage. They act amused that I speak Spanish, but not so amused they don't throw me in jail. The cell feels like being in an animal stall. The floor is concrete with straw scattered about. There is a bowl of water with a cup, a one-foot by two-foot barred opening in the wall for ventilation, and a bucket to pee in. Food, I can only expect to be an unwelcome surprise. I ask the guard how long until we can negotiate my release for drinking on the sidewalk. He says he needs to ask his sergeant, who was not there. The reality of spending the night here terrifies me. I try to get comfortable, an impossible task. Gathering handfuls of straw, I stuff the scratchy stuff behind my back and lean against the wall facing the window for ventilation. My situation is scary, but not life threatening. This will only take a little more time I think, and time is what I have.

Later that evening, the cell doors open. My first thought is that I'm going to be released, but I'm not so lucky. They put two men into the cell. Now I'm scared. Have you ever been with a dog when he senses someone he does not trust? That was me, sensing that mistrust. Both men were American and appeared intoxicated. One skinny and tall, wearing tight blue jeans, and cowboy boots. He appeared to be in control. The other one is short with only half an arm, his body movements fast and jittery. He also wore cowboy boots and jeans, was unshaven, with baggy ill-fitting clothes. Both men were loud and angry, cursing at the jail guard in English and repeatably saying fucking Mexicans, fucking Mexicans.

Later, they take an interest in me when I begin talking with the guard. The guard kept asking me questions about "Free Love"; he thought everyone in the states were having sex everywhere, all the time, with everyone. The tall skinny one says, "If you speak Spanish, can you get us out of here?"

The short man continues to wad up straw, throwing it against the wall, and cursing. I told him, when the guard comes over, I will ask him what it will take to get us out. After getting the guards' attention and asking what it will take, he responds *esperas* (wait). Without talking to his sergeant, he asks how quickly we want out? We want out now, I tell him, all three of us, not just them, I add, not missing my opportunity to escape.

The guard came back with an offer of $5000. Pricey, I thought, but being seventeen, anything over $100 sounds expensive. The tall skinny man is not pleased, but removes one cowboy boot, extracts a wad of money and counts out $5000. It looks to me as if he has at least double that amount, which he returns to his boot. Handing me $5000 and saying "Do it" in an unpleasant voice. I've seen a lot of cop shows on television and this is how they do it. This better work out. I carry the money over to the cell door and explain how we want this to happen. Simple, no other people in the room, no drama. I tell him the money will be handed over on our way out the door, and he agrees with a big smile, his mouth almost drooling. As he is the only one there, he can pocket the total amount. A moment later, the exchange is made. We are out. Wow! I have just negotiated myself out of a Mexican jail and am still alive to tell the story.

As we walk out the door, and I'm about ready to say goodbye, the tall skinny man asks me, "Where are you going?"

"To the bus station," I reply.

"Wrong. You're not going anywhere."

Standing straight, trying not to show my fear, I ask, "What do you mean?"

"You're coming with us. We need to be in Lake Chapala outside of Guadalajara tomorrow and you are going to get us there."

Referring back in my mind to all the police shows I've seen, I think I know what can happen if I don't follow through. It is a sixteen-hour drive. He had money and I could pull this off by finding a car and driver. The two men stood over me and said, "Agree?"

Responding without hesitation, I said, "Yes."

The one-armed man said, "Let's get this going."

It doesn't take me long to find an independent taxi driver, who tells us he needs to find a second driver for such a long trip. The driver said he would return in an hour. He showed up on time with his *tio* (uncle) to help drive. We still had to negotiate the details; figuring the cost of gas and labor, the taxi driver settles on $125,000 pesos or $500 American dollars. Their body language says they're not impressed with my deal making but when they see the large car, a Ford Galaxy that we all fit into, the tall man nods.

The short one-armed man shouts, "You tell that son of a bitch, he's going to do whatever I say. If I have to take a piss he's going to stop, if I'm hungry or want a beer he is to stop, got it? And his friend will sit and shut up. I don't want to hear a lot of fucking Spanish radio or talking while driving."

His loud, aggressive voice frightens me, and, I say "I hear you."

My intuition is that the Mexican taxi driver knows what is going on and agrees to these conditions to protect me. This scheme has to work out, or I'll be in trouble or dead.

We leave that afternoon. The two drivers ride in the front seat, while the three of us squeeze into the back. With five men in the car, the air-conditioning did not work as well as we would have liked. We traveled for a few hours when the short-armed man suddenly swung his half arm, hitting the driver in the back of the head and shouting, "Stop now!"

The driver spoke no English. Since the driver spoke no English, I jumped in and directed the driver, in Spanish, to pull over. The short man exited the car and peed on the side of the road, which was legal in Mexico. Back in the car, I asked the short guy to ask me first next time, so I could translate for him. He brushed me off and did the same thing a couple more times before morning.

Eventually we pulled into the town of Tepic. We were not taking the most direct route. The driver had told me privately the shorter route was not as good, with few places to turn off, and we were safer driving though Tepic and tracking back a short distance. I did not relay this information to the Texans as I only aspired to be on the safest road. We were all hungry and ready for breakfast. I chose a very public place, where they could not cause a scene. We sat down, one table for the three of us and the two drivers choosing a table away from us. The skinny guy got my attention and told me to keep my eye on the drivers and "don't let them go anywhere." He leaned over, lifted his pant leg above his boot, exposing a small pistol strapped to his leg. The gun stunned me, and I got his point immediately. I walked over and told the drivers to order what they want. If the drivers knew about the gun, they would ditch us, leaving me to answer. The waiter came to the table and asked for our order, and I responded in Spanish to let him know someone spoke his language.

Without knowing what was on the menu, the short man blurted out, "Two eggs, bacon, and toast. No fucking beans or fucking tortillas."

I translated the order minus the vulgar language. The tall guy would have the same. Not the typical breakfast order in Mexico. I worked it out with the waiter and hoped their food came out the way the men wanted. They kept silent until the food arrived. The short guy looked at the bacon, which in Mexico is prepared a little fatty and less cooked than they were accustomed to, then he looked at the bacon and threw it on the floor. The waiter jumped in to resolve the problem. I apologized and asked if he could bring another bacon order but crispy. He brought a new order out, and things settled down while we ate. When we finished eating, the disgruntled Texans paid the bill with my help.

Back on the road. Riding with two nasty men with a guns strapped to their legs made it worse, even though I was sure the gun was for the drivers, not for me. Still, this gun could be for anyone. Guadalajara was another six to eight hours, including another frightful lunch. The short guy ordered tacos but wanted bread, not tortillas. After some confusion, one of the drivers spoke up and told the vendor to put the taco ingredients on pan bimbo, the Mexican version of white Wonder bread.

After several more unexpected road stops to pee and buy beer, we came closer and closer to ending our trip to Guadalajara. I became happier and happier to still be alive.

We arrived in Guadalajara in the afternoon. Lake Chapala is another thirty miles south of town. Never having been there, I don't know what to expect but as we approach Lake Chapala, I see a well-to-do area, with ranches and estates lining the lakeshore. We come to a gated entrance and wait while the iron gates open for us to pass. We drive through the manicured entrance and head down a long driveway to the house. A well-dressed man in his forties greets us. After getting our bags, the Texans told the two drivers to go on their way. I'd been planning to hitch a ride with them into town but then the men invite me to spend the night. I don't like these men, but as I'm still alive and curious, so I agreed. The ranch was complete with lawns, colorful gardens, exotic animals, and pets, including horses, llamas, and alpacas. A half a dozen men and women are working the gardens, landscaping, and tending to the horses and animals. Inside the large house, they show me to my room, where I stay until dinner. After dinner, everyone seemed to disappear. Exhausted, I went to sleep.

The next morning, I wake up frightened and regretting my decision to spend the night. Feeling vulnerable and clearly in over my head I plan to ask for a ride into town to catch the bus to Mexico City.

The kitchen staff hand me coffee and cup in hand, I wander through the house and come upon a library or study. A book on the history of the state of Jalisco catches my attention and I begin to read.

Later, the Texans enter the room, and we go into the dining room for breakfast. I build up the courage to ask for a ride to town and they say someone will take me to town after lunch. Relieved, I excuse myself and start towards the door. The short man stops me, asking if I want to go horseback riding. I was content just looking around, so I said nothing. He lit a joint and said, "Let's ride the fucking horses."

What choice did I have? I said yes. We left the house and headed towards the barn. Several workers saddle two horses, and off we go. He appears to know how to ride and asks me if I have ever ridden before?

"Yes, I have," I said.

We ride until we come to a small outbuilding. Four or five small men of Indian descent were standing around. The one-armed short man looked down at the men and starts to laugh. Wild laughter, the laughter you hear from someone who has been smoking marijuana and is the only one who knows the joke. A laugh that didn't stop. The Indian men look confused but try to be polite by joining in with the laughter. The short guy jumped off his horse, shouting, "No one laughs at me," heads towards the men and begins pushing, hitting, and kicking them. The hitting turns into a bloody beating. He was hurting them. I was horrified to see a man beat like that but felt helpless to intervene. I move my horse away from the other horses, and wait until, finally, the short man mounts his horse. We are about to leave when my horse spooks and takes off at a full gallop. Pulling back on the reins, kicking, and screaming, nothing I do will stop the horse. The horse makes a sudden turn, heads toward a forested area, and brushes me off on a tree. I hit the ground hard, pain setting in immediately. The one-armed guy rides up, looks down at me in disgust and says, "I thought you could ride." Then he rode off for help, saying he'd be back soon. Sitting on the ground in excruciating pain, I await his return.

When I see an ambulance coming across the field, I become wary. I had heard that Mexican ambulances are unreliable. I'm worried that I'll receive unprofessional care and be treated at a second-class health facility. I felt that recognizable feeling of being in trouble again. But when the ambulance arrives and two men jump out to attend to me, I see that one of them is an American doctor with an assistant. He splints my leg, loads me into the ambulance, and we're off to the hospital. During the trip, he explains that there is an American medical school and a teaching hospital in Guadalajara and that I will get excellent treatment.

We pull into the hospital and I'm wheeled into a room where I am examined, have blood drawn and x-rays taken, before any paperwork is done. Later, the same doctor came in and explained that I had no broken bones. My leg had a nasty bruise and pulled muscles but it would recover on its own. We talked for a while, and I gave him my history. He thought I was crazy traveling by myself with epilepsy. He wanted to call my parents since I was only seventeen. I pleaded with the doctor not to call. My mother would want me to come home. I had a plan and there is no going back. He asked me to stay another day and rest my leg. I agreed but let him know I had little money. He said we'd worry about that later.

As the doctor requested, I spent another day in the hospital worrying about the hospital bill and how long my leg would be out of commission, while hoping the doctor hadn't betrayed me and called my parents. The next morning, the doctor came in, checked my leg, and told me I could go, although my leg would not be one hundred percent for over a week. Again, he asked about my plans, and I told him about my experiences with my uncle and where I had been. Hearing that I had a support system relaxed him and he fixed me up with first-aid items, a crutch and pain medication, then filled my seizure prescription with an extra month of medicine. I was still unsure about who was paying for everything, but the doctor explained that in Mexico, emergency medical care was free except for the hospital room and that someone from administration would talk to me. A nice and compassionate woman who spoke English brought paperwork in and explained that someone had come and paid for everything in full. They had also left me an envelope. I gathered my bag and headed out the door, waiting for a taxi to the bus station. In the taxi, I opened the envelope, and found six-hundred dollars in cash and a note. The note read: "Everything has been taken care of and never return." If we had been in person, I would have said: "DON'T WORRY. I WON'T."

I never knew what was going on at that ranch, but I believe it had to do with the Mexican drug cartel.

Chapter 7

The Monkey and Me

Wanting to avoid the congested traffic in Mexico City, which is difficult because almost all roads lead there, I headed south on the bus from Guadalajara towards my destination, Chiapas. We passed through Toluca, a mountainous town outside the valley or bowl of Mexico City. An ancient Aztec city, Toluca has a tradition celebrating the Day of the Dead and patron saints. Toluca celebrates every patron saint, which makes for a celebration for every calendar day of the year. Toluca itself was too busy for me. So, I headed ten miles south to the small town of Metepec, an artsy town known for its crafts and artists. I found a place to stay for under one dollar per night and wandered into the town square.

Employing my usual method when arriving in a new town, I sit down for a shoeshine and to ask the boys what's happening in town as they seem to know everything that is going on. Within five minutes, a large spider monkey, probably someone's pet, sashays across the park, sits down next to me and stares into my face. I talk to the monkey like you would talk to a dog. The conversation was one-way until the monkey grabs onto my leg, thankfully not the leg I had recently injured. After a few minutes, I try to get up and leave. This is not a small monkey you might see at a pet store; it is probably four feet tall when standing. I reach down and grab the monkey's hand to remove it from my leg, but he snatches my hand and shoves it into his mouth, biting down gently to signal that he is not letting go. I try to lift his hand again and get the same reaction. Looking over at the shoeshine boys, I say, "Quita el chango" (Get rid of this monkey).

But they just laugh, finding the whole thing hilarious. On the street in front of us, a crowd was forming. Again, I call out, "Quita el chango," and the monkey holds on tight.

I ask the shoeshine boys, "What should I do?"

Apparently, I am not the first person this monkey has befriended in this way. They tell me that the owner is a little girl, and the only one who could remove the monkey.

"Okay, where is this little girl?"

The boy said she was in school. I convinced one of the boys to go to the school and ask the girl's teacher if she could come help. We waited about twenty minutes, as the crowd grew larger, with at least ten people gawking at me suspiciously as if it was my fault. Finally, I saw a little girl headed towards us with one of the shoeshine boys. Finally, the girl takes the monkey's hand and unfolds it from my leg, apologizing as she leads him away. I tip the shoeshine boys and go on my way.

I wander around town for a few more hours, eat some food, listen to some good traditional Mexican music, and retire to my lodging, I am surprised to find a full meal waiting for me as I hadn't figured that for one dollar a night, I'd also get dinner. Sitting down with the family, we eat and talk about the history of the area. The mother tells me that the Otomi tribe had once lived in the Tula valley where Mexico City is now. After the Aztec empire and the Nahua Indian tribe took most of their land, the remaining Otomi people moved up into the mountains. This became Metepec. Then, when the Spaniards arrived in the 1500s, they enslaved the Otomi people using their labor to mine silver. Until Mexico gained independence from Spain, most of the Otomi land and culture had all been forgotten. Now Metepec had several festivals every year to celebrate the rich history of their culture. I told her and her husband and two children that having dinner and spending the night felt like home. I was thankful to them for dinner and the history lesson.

The next morning, I was off to Chiapas. First, though, I added two days to my trip by taking the bus to Jalapa to say goodbye to Lucy and the family, thanking them for all they had given me. This was important for me to do before leaving for Chiapas. I had lunch with Lucy; we talk about the good times we had together and with Uncle Bill. I tell Lucy my plans to go to Sitala and say "Adios" to the family, thanking them again for everything. Later, I spend the night at a friend's house in Jalapa.

To Mexico City

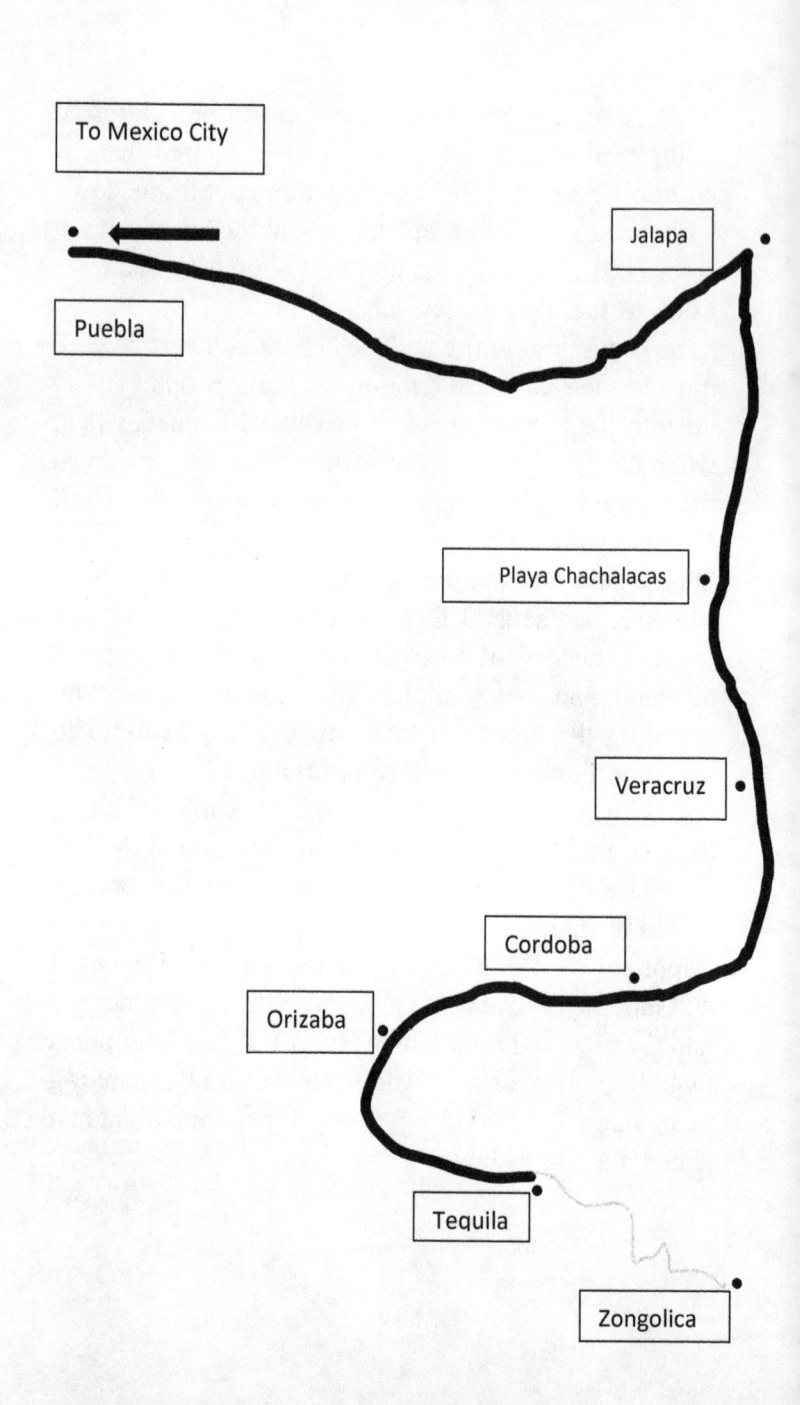

Puebla

Jalapa

Playa Chachalacas

Veracruz

Cordoba

Orizaba

Tequila

Zongolica

Chapter 8

Side Trip to Zongolica

Leaving Jalapa, I take a side trip to a small village called Zongolica, that I visited with Uncle Bill on our mission trip. This region fascinated me, and I want to learn more about the *brujos* (witches) in the area. I had learned enough of the dialect, Nahuatl, to get by when I traveled with Uncle Bill, and we visited brujos' homes, but not a cave.

At the open market, I ask how I can meet with a brujo. They direct me to the herb stalls where I meet an older Indian woman dressed in colorful embroidered ethnic clothing, with many markings indicating witchcraft. She asks what I need, and I tell her I only want to understand more about the witchcraft practices of the area. We agree to meet at the herb stall the next morning. The one instruction she gives me is to not eat any breakfast. When I ask about a cleansing, she says it is the first step in my ability to understand. I know that their rituals include dancing, washing with herbs and ash from sacrificed animals and listening to music in smoke-filled huts, and I look forward to the morning with both anticipation and trepidation. The only negative thing I know about their witchcraft is that the Catholics in the area fear many of their practices, which involve animal sacrifice, and people would leave church when a brujo entered. That night, I eat an enormous meal, knowing there will be no breakfast. The next morning, I meet the woman and another man at the herb stall, in the darkest corner of the market. This area also contains the old-style Indian medicine section and the religious and magical practices stalls, some of which date back to pre-Columbian times, thousands of years ago. These traditional and ancient medical rituals are still popular today, with many people using them prior to seeing a medical doctor using Western medicine.

This dark corner of the market seems mysterious. The stall is crowded with wooden crates, baskets, primitive shelving, tables and items hanging from the ceiling: dried avocado leaves for heart health, dried snakes as cancer medication, dried skunks to strengthen the blood, chains of garlic to ward off evil, and deer's eyes to protect against an evil eye. Other plants, animal parts and insects are for sale to be used in medical and spiritual potions. The woman gathers a few herbs and a large bag of different tree barks and directs me to a rickety second-class bus.

As a skinny white boy with curly red hair falling below my shoulders, following an older Indian woman everyone knew was a witch, I must stand out. The second-class bus is full of pigs, goats, chickens, food of every type, and people of every age, music playing and children dancing. We went only a few miles to a lake, where we get off and walk to the shore. Cliffs border the lake about thirty feet from the water's edge. We enter a damp candle lit cave with a large wood and stone altar at the back. The altar is maybe twenty feet long, decorated with both human and animal bones, horns, dead and alive animals, birds in cages, insects, shells, dried fish, feathers, eggs, hair, candles, and amulets of every description. There were pictures of shamans as well as men, women, children, and religious icons of saints. Masks made of wood and clay representing animals like pigs, eagles, snakes, armadillos and so on were hanging everywhere. The altar is also full of masks of devils, deformed humans, and half human- half animal beings. The smell of the cave is foul and pungent like a mix of herbs, and the odor of an old dirt basement floor. She gathers some large eggs she tells me are turkey eggs, and some liquid in small bottles. I cannot understand what she tells me about the small bottles. She keeps speaking about the cleansing and preparing for different sacrifices or offerings. The liquid has a brown, green color. Before we leave the cave, she takes some short tree branches she gathered at the market. The brujo or male witch was younger than the bruja, maybe in his late thirties, wearing a fedora hat, sandals, and a floral shirt. He has no more authority than the bruja, they seem to be equals. He selects a piece of wood and scrapes some bark from it and puts it in a small pouch.

We're there about a half an hour when we finally exit the cave into blinding morning light outside. The woman directs me to several mud-walled huts with reed roofs. We enter one of the huts, and she asks me to sit, explaining that I need to be *limpia* (clean) before we talk further. The brujo mixed the brown, green liquid with some of the wood shavings. It looks like an herbal tea.

He asks me to remove my shirt, shoes, and socks and hands me the tea-colored liquid to drink. Within five minutes, I can hear and see, but my body feels ice cold and I am scared. I try, but I cannot move. The brujo places several of the turkey eggs on my stomach, and rolls them back and forth across my chest, stomach, and legs. Then he and the bruja sprinkle crushed bones on my chest. Finally, he puts on a mask of a deformed animal and begins to chant. The chanting is loud and slow, with a strange pitch alternating between high and low. They leave me alone in the hut with four or five bowls of bark burning, filling the air with a smokey haze. The hut has no door, only a two-foot by five-foot opening, allowing enough smoke to escape to keep me from being overwhelmed. Later that evening, a different woman enters with cooked eggs and spoon feeds me, as if I am a small, sick child. Before leaving, she takes a flat piece of wood and lays hair from the back of my head on a wood plank. With a knife, she chops off a handful of my curls. She leaves me overnight with a blanket for warmth.

In the morning, the brujo and bruja come back. She says the *limpiad* or cleansing is almost complete. The brujo burns more herbs, and sprinkles more of the crushed bones on my chest along with ashes he collects from the tree bark he burnt the day before. I am frightened, not knowing how long this will continue. I am not hallucinating or feeling high on drugs, no pain, just lying on a wooden bench. I was being fed but am still hungry.

Zongolica was not a center for witchcraft. I chose it because it is far enough away from Catemaco that I could experience a more ancient, authentic form of witchcraft. Still, I had not expected to be drugged and kept in a mud hut for days. My plan had been to spend a day researching witchcraft in this area of Veracruz. Instead, although I am not hurt physically, mentally I am driving myself crazy with worry about what they were doing. Perhaps they saw me having a seizure and this fascinated them. Maybe they thought the *limpiad* or cleansing would control the seizures and, if not, they would keep on trying with different sorcery and witchcraft. My mind is clear enough that I know I need to leave yet I remain there, lying on an old wooden slab because I cannot get up. No one knows I am here. I hadn't left an itinerary with anyone because itineraries were not my style.

I want to write something to let my family know I had not forgotten them. At the same time, I believe I can handle this and will somehow get out of this mess. Somehow.

Eventually, on the third afternoon, a couple named Sara and Tom, vacationing from New Zealand, stumble across me in the mud hut. I explain my predicament and they agree to help me. Getting out of there is not easy. I have not stood for several days, I've eaten very little and am under some kind of spell, hypnotized or immobilized by some herb. Tom and Sara help me up and then stand by me while I adjust to being on my feet again. Listening to my story, and then noticing where my hair is missing, they become quite alarmed. We find my backpack with all my stuff still there. As we talk more, I tell them where I'm going, and they insist I see a doctor before continuing my trip. I agree and together we move out of the hut.

Their car is about a mile away. Though weakened, I am still young and strong, and am able to walk with help. My pants are so loose that I hold them up with one hand as we walk along the dirt path, fearful the brujos would come after me. Looking behind me as we walk, I see someone watching us, but when I turn around again, they are gone. Finally, we get to the car. By that time, whatever had paralyzed me was wearing off. There were doctors in Catemaco, but that city is too close to the center of witchcraft for me right then. I convinced my new friends to drive to Tuxtla, only fifty miles away. I had been there and knew the town was big enough for us to find a doctor. Tom and Sarah's car is a late model Saab filled with their belongings. With a great deal of organizing, I fit in with my backpack. Tom was the most cautious driver I had ever driven with, and he turned a one-hour drive into two hours. Arriving in Tuxtla, we found a doctor and agreed to meet at the hospital. After examining me, the doctor said I had lost some weight and was dehydrated and needed some real nourishment but otherwise I was okay. I thanked him, then took time to discuss my seizures with him. He was not a neurologist and urged me to stay on my prescribed medication. He said I was lucky. If I had been stuck in that hut much longer, with the brujos believing they could clean the seizures from me, I could have wasted away. Afterward Tom, Sarah, and I had dinner, and together we looked at their maps, and I give them some suggestions of places to visit. I kept thanking them for saving me. Then I was back on the road again, towards Oaxaca.

Chapter 9

To Oaxaca

While I was home in California, friends were interested in where I had been, and suggested places to visit and things to do there. The most popular, to get high on psilocybin. Psychedelic mushrooms like psilocybin are native to Mexico, in the state of Oaxaca. Along the Mexican coast, nestled in a pine forest, is the town San Jose del Pacifico. When Rolling Stone Magazine wrote that Bob Dylan and John Lennon showed up there to experiment with mushrooms this small town became popular.

San Jose del Pacifico shares the Pacific coast with Acapulco and other touristy resort towns, which I had no interest in. In Tuxtla I was told that the same mushrooms found along the coast are native to the Huautla mountains, and I believed that taking mushrooms with native Indians in Huautla would be a better experience than in the mushroom mecca of San Jose del Pacifico.

I left Tuxtla for Oaxaca, taking a direct route over the Huautla mountains rather than going around them. The road was part broken asphalt, part dirt, and part mud, which I figured had to be more interesting and adventurous than traveling on the freeway. There was no road connecting both sides of the mountain. Instead, once I arrived in Oaxaca City, I would have to then take a different, second-class bus back up that side of the mountain to Huautla.

The bus traveled this road twice a week. Besides the men, women and children, and chickens, there were goats, pigs and dogs loaded onto the back of the bus. Along with a few noisy roosters, the hens were crackling and causing a fuss the entire trip. We'd been on the road for an hour when an older Indian woman, carrying a basket of belongings and eggs, rose from her seat, grasping the metal railing above to keep her balance on the curving bumpy road. At the front of the bus, she shouted to the driver to stop. When he didn't pull over, she began hitting him with a small stick, still shouting. "*Tletl Tletl*" Stop! Stop! Eventually, the driver pulled over, stepped off the bus, and walked to the back with the persistent old woman. The driver opened the door, and the woman reached into the bus and collected an egg. I was amazed. How did this woman recognize from all those noisy chickens that it was her hen that had laid an egg while riding on a bumpy mountain road in an old raggedy bus?

We continued over the mountains which ranged from 1000 feet to 8000 feet in elevation. The road was wet, rocky, and muddy. As we approached the top of the mountain, the bus got stuck in the mud. The driver braked, and ordered everyone out, including the pets and animals. People exited calmly as if they knew the routine and understood what was coming next. As the women and children herded the animals, trying their best to contain them on the side of the road, the men gathered behind the bus with shovels and began to dig the bus out of the mud. Then we pushed, me included.

Ce, Ome, Ye, Maxopehua—One, Two, Three, Push! We worked in rhythm, the men pushing with the chanting and pushing continuing for some time. Men digging and men pushing, and men holding rocks to be used as blocks then jamming the rocks behind the tires each time, preventing the bus from rolling backwards. Small in stature but big in determination and strength, the men followed this method until they reached the top of the hill, a distance of about fifty feet. Every man gave one-hundred percent effort while maintaining smiles on their faces.

While the men worked, the women prepared a meal. Rather than a lunch box, workers carried half of a gourd like a small bowl. The meal was cornmeal, sugar, and other grains mixed to form a simple porridge, or *nemiliz tlacualli*. The children went into the forest to collect native sweet fruits from the mountains. Before eating, the men spent a half an hour thanking the women and children for the meal. Standing on the side of that dirt road, I noticed how polite and kind they were to one another. They told stories and reminisced about the past. Telling stories was common when meeting in a group. They had little to talk about other than their lives, no radios, no television, no newspaper, no news from beyond five miles of where they lived. They did not tie their stories to time; the events seemed to have no beginning or end. We stood in a group, stirring the mixture and eating with our fingers. I felt special to be there sharing a meal with them.

After *nepantlayot,* or lunch, we loaded the animals back onto the bus. Quite a funny ordeal since not all the animals were cooperative. Children wrestled with the goats and sheep and struggled collecting chickens. Finally, everyone took their seats, and we were off again, now a half day behind schedule. The rest of the trip was downhill with no interruptions. No one was upset with the delay. No one had a clock, only daylight and darkness. Some people began singing to the sound of an old beat-up guitar and other native instruments. Women talked and stitched on cloth, children played, and chickens laid eggs. We pulled into Oaxaca City in the evening, first stopping by the marketplace to unload the animals which would be sold in the morning. The bus continued on to the station and we all got off, saying *"cualli onnenwmictiliiol,"* not goodbye, but "peaceful travels" as we each went our own ways. Markets were closing, people were getting off work, the daytime life was ending and the nighttime life getting started. I asked around and found a single room to spend the night and take a shower, which I needed after digging the bus out of the mud.

Oaxaca is the capital city of the state of Oaxaca, on the border of the Aztec and Mayan cultures and has the largest diversity of Indian cultures in Mexico. Nowhere was this clearer than in the open markets and streets. Both young and old women wore colorful dresses, skirts, and blouses. The colors, weave patterns, and hand-stitched designs represented different tribes and cultures. Men's clothing was less colorful, white pants and shirts, and huaraches for footwear. Teenagers and young adults wore denim and cotton shirts, adopting more western culture in their attire. Music was playing in the market, small groups of men gathered at different sections of the market playing music that represented the many Mexican and Indian cultures in the area. Mariachi music playing on one corner, Indian men playing flutes, small guitars, and violins in another corner.

I headed out of town on a bus to visit the cultural museum and ruins of Monte Alban, only forty minutes away. The Zapotecs Indians built Monte Alban around 1500 BC. This archeological site was discovered in 1930 on a fifty-seven-acre plateau overlooking a valley. When I arrived, archeologists from Purdue University were working on-site along with some early onlookers. I talked with students working there and learned that this massive stone city, its structures reaching four to eight stories high, was built without beasts of burden. These were stone structures built by hand. Wherever I looked rocks were engraved with holographic symbols, which were used to tell ancestors' stories and show the history of their culture. Wanting to learn more about this history and the decline of Monte Alban, I spent hours climbing on the structures. The stone ruins were still being cleaned, studied, and understood., and I was free to roam.

In Oaxaca, a local man staying next to my room told me he had lived in Oaxaca his entire life; as a boy he and his friends ran around, finding hundreds of objects that are now considered valuable and protected. Later, this man gave me directions to the second-class bus stop to buy a ticket to the village of Huautla.

My other option would have been taking the "vomit van" to San Jose del Pacifico with the tourists. My bus trip to the mountains was longer, but eating "Niño's de Santos," or fresh mushrooms, sounded more inviting than taking Greenies, the processed mushrooms reserved for tourists. The vomit van provided transportation to and from Oaxaca and San Jose Del Pacifico, travelling fast on winding roads and causing passengers to vomit. No, thank you!

Chapter 10

The Land of Magic Mushrooms

I ride the bus for three to four hours arriving in Huautla, a village similar to others I had visited: a small central plaza surrounded by dirt paths, with a small *tienda* or store selling sodas, cooking oil, kerosene, aspirin, and some general dry goods. Off to one side is a concrete block and wood structure with a corrugated sheet metal roof to house a small clinic that has its own generator. The generator powers one light in the clinic and two or three lights in the plaza. That is all the electricity for the entire village. There is no running water or sewer. There is a hand pump station and a fast-moving creek for water. Not even an outhouse, just two seats positioned over a cliff. Below, pigs gathered and ate the waste. Toilet paper is available, although it was a thin tree bark that came off in sheets not unlike birch bark. It worked well. The Indians in this area are of Mazatec descent, which covers a wide diversity of tribes throughout Oaxaca. Nahautha is the dialect spoken here. We are only forty miles as birds fly from Zongolica and the dialect spoken there overlapped with the dialect spoken in the mountains.

I was both eager and apprehensive about trying out this psychedelic experience. I had experimented with LSD back in California and peyote in Mexico; my seizures were not a problem then and I do not expect a problem now. A short and fragile seeming woman approached and directed me to a one room hut with a thatched roof and dirt floor. The room was empty except for an elevated wooden platform to both sleep and sit on, and the dirt floor was covered in pine needles to keep insects away. I say thank you in Nahautl, *Tlazocamati,* put down my stuff and pull out a piece of paper to write any unfamiliar words to add to my vocabulary. The pronunciation, including many gutturals and clicking sounds, is more difficult than learning the meaning of the word.

The woman I met earlier offered me food, a small, thick tortilla with beans and a tasty beet-like root. I venture outside and walk around. A very tall man, wearing a button-down shirt and speaking some Spanish approached and invited me to his home. His broken Spanish was mixed with Nahautl, and we communicated the best we were able. I asked about the local crops, schooling, and the small clinic. He told me that the children had school, where they learned manners, cultural rules, farming, simple math, and Spanish. He explained that people went to the market in Oaxaca several times a year, bringing handcrafts the women make and fruits that are only found in the mountains. The clinic has a doctor or nurse who stop in once or twice per month to check in on the children and elderly, and to give vaccines and classes on diet and health. We toasted with a kind of liquor, which tasted like mead, made from honey. Before I left, he asked if I came to partake in eating hungos or Ninos de Santo. I said yes, and he responded, with a smile, "In the morning."

The next morning, I wake up early and wander through the village. Children are everywhere and gather around me. I go back to my hut, pull out my frisbee and play with them until their mothers call them for breakfast and school. Soon after, two elderly women arrive at my hut. One woman opens a large leaf she is carrying to show me a pair of very thin hungos, bluish-green mushrooms that are covered with the morning dew.

I thank the women and sat down in my hut to think about what I was doing. Is this why I came to Mexico? Uncle Bill is now in Brazil, my support system is gone, I have only myself to get advice from. I have dropped out of school, my family is three thousand miles away, yet I have a strong feeling this is where I need to be. Prior to being in Mexico, I was controlled and directed by my parents, psychiatrists, psychologists, and therapists. This time in Mexico is my opportunity to prove to myself I can navigate life successfully on my own. I feel comfortable being totally on my own, making my own decisions. People here have been taking these mushrooms for thousands of years. There is nothing to fear. Like LSD and peyote, they are psychedelics that distort time and space. This was a safe space, and I planned to enjoy this experience. Even so, I am nervous that my seizure medication might interact, but I wasn't about to let that stop me.

It's cool in the mountains, and I slip on a long sleeve shirt, grab a container of water, eat the mushrooms, and go for a walk in the old growth forest. A half hour later the mushrooms kick in. The color of the wildflowers intensifies, and they appear larger than before. The reds are redder, greens greener and blues bluer. Birds are singing as if it is a concert. I come upon a fast-moving creek and watch the water as it tumbles and splashes over rocks, that same movement mirrors in my body. I continue walking along a narrow, wet path through the forest, occasionally passing smiling people carrying firewood. I stand still and watch trees sway in the wind. Later, I lie down in a forest opening, looking up and wondering what others have experienced in this peaceful space. I feel as if I'm floating on a raft, without a single worry. After several hours, the Ninos de Santos wear off and I walked back to the village.

When I return, Matzi, the man I met earlier, invites me to share a meal at his home. He has a simple pine table with four primitive chairs and a bed; Matzi invited me to sit. He offered me *pulque*, a special liqueur, reserved only for guests. Pulque is an ancient alcoholic drink, milk-colored and foamy, made from the fermented sap of the agave plant. Pulque tastes like beer that is in the process of fermenting, with a touch of tequila. The drink is an acquired taste. Politely, I sip on the milky liquid. We share a traditional dinner of a squash dish with a small portion of chicken and a corn patty like a small fat tortilla.

The next day I spend with Matzi. He tells me that Ninos de Santos is part of a ceremony recognizing *Nahualli*, an Aztec word meaning "Shadow Soul." It is your animal twin, your spiritual double. The Aztecs viewed animals as sacred beings that dwelled among the gods. These gods sent messages to humans via animals. If a particular bird or animal would cross your path, you would often consult a shaman for help to interpret this omen. On the fourth day of a child's life, a shaman or priest would perform a ritual, joining the human soul with the Nahualli for life. According to Matzi, we can understand Nahualli best under the influence of Ninos de Santos.

Matzi emphasized that getting high on psilocybin was not a daily event. He was concerned that Ninos de Santos was not being respected by tourists and people outside of the mountains. I assure him I respect his culture and beliefs. We talk about how the Mazatec Indians' ways are disappearing, and he tells me he'd never thought it would be necessary to teach the children to speak Spanish, but it has happened. Matzi was so genuine and spoke earnestly about his people, his fears and hopes for the Mazatec Indians. One of the most articulate and inspirational men I have ever met, he was filled with pride for his people and a deep understanding of the role his culture played in Mexican life. My time with Matzi was completely in the present, he never asked me where I was from or what I was doing, nor did he tell me what he was doing in Huautla.

There was nothing to prove, I had only to be myself right where we were.

Map of the Yucatán Peninsula

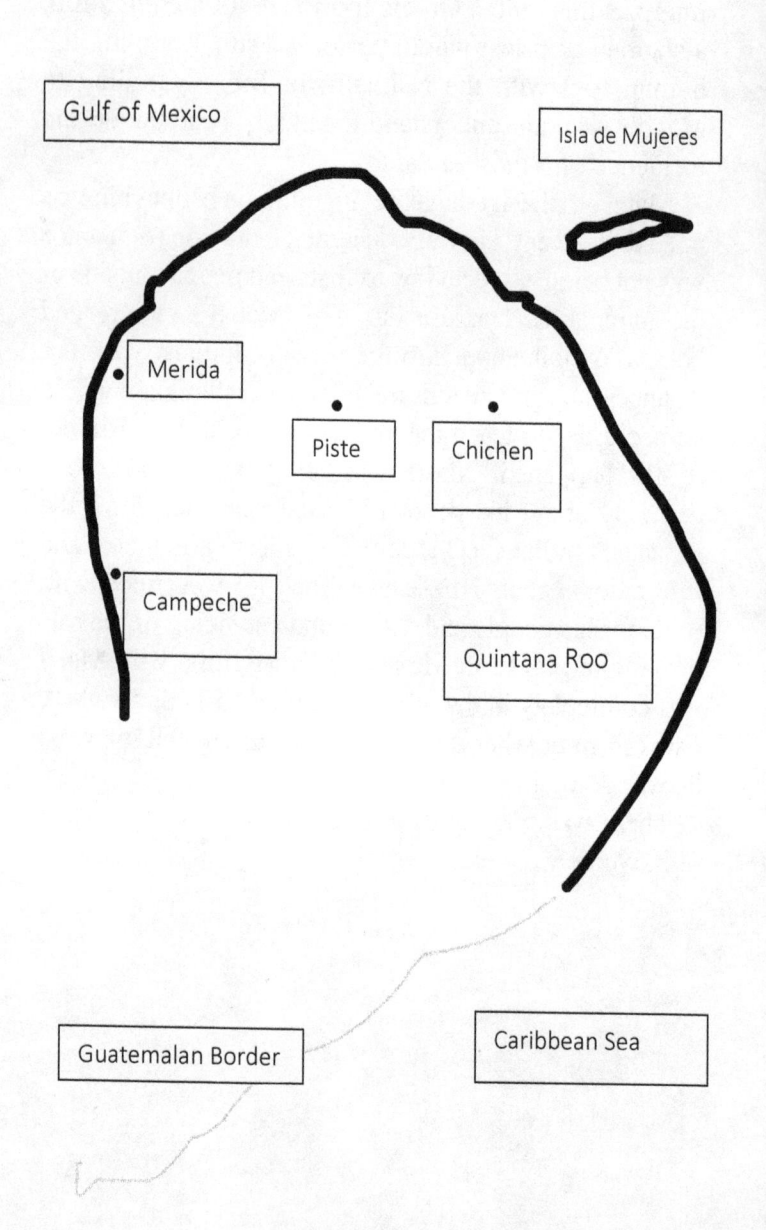

- Gulf of Mexico
- Isla de Mujeres
- Merida
- Piste
- Chichen
- Campeche
- Quintana Roo
- Guatemalan Border
- Caribbean Sea

Chapter 11

Off to an Island

After partaking in Ninos de Santos, I routed myself from Oaxaca to the Yucatan Peninsula and the Isla de Mujeres. Oaxaca borders the Pacific Ocean; Yucatan borders the Gulf of Mexico on the eastern side of the country. Wanting to visit Edzna and Calakmul, I left Huatla for the city of Campeche.

Campeche, an ancient coastal fortress built during the invasion of the Spanish in 1500, still stands today. European architecture is prevalent, and buildings and homes are decorative and festive. Painted in reds, greens, pinks, and blues, the town looks like a bouquet of flowers.

In Campeche I rent a hammock on the beach for fifty cents a night, tying the hammock between two palm trees. The temperature is in the high seventies with a cool breeze, perfect sleeping weather. The next morning, I meet a couple of men on the beach and share some sweet breads and fruit from a street vendor for breakfast, standing on the sidewalk. After our meal the two men, who were heading to work, asked if I wanted to join them to work for a day. Having a bit of extra money would be helpful, so I accepted their offer. The work paid twelve pesos or about one dollar per hour. My job was cleaning engine parts, using a combination of diesel fuel and kerosene. The work was smelly, dirty, and hard, but interesting. I lasted only two days. The men just joked around all day talking shit. On the second day, after work, they invited me to a cantina. The bar was an old building on a dirt road with no sign. On the walls were old calendars with bullfighters on the covers. I figured out that you can tell if an old bar is any good by how many calendars are hanging on the walls.

At the end of the bar, a cooked pig's head, with the top of the skull missing was impaled on a wooden spike. Next to it were small forks, toothpicks, tortillas, pico de gallo and hot sauce. Not knowing the way to pick at a pig's head, I waited and watched. One of my new friends approached the end of the bar, he picked up a tortilla, folded it over, grasped a loose piece of meat on the pig's head, dunked it in the pico with a splash of hot sauce, and shoved it into his mouth. I didn't know why we needed the forks until another man grabbed a tortilla, and a fork and picked at the white fleshy brains. Finally, I was ready to indulge. A unique dish, *"muy sabroso"* flavorful.

Feeling good with a few extra pesos in my pocket, I headed off deeper into the Yucatan peninsula, towards the archeological sites of Edzna and Calakmul. The year was 1971, and these sites were discovered thirty years earlier. At the site several men and women were cleaning and photographing stone images and hieroglyphic writings. I'd been to many Mayan and Aztec ruins in the past few years. Sometimes they looked similar, but I always learned something new from the men and women working on site. Translating inscriptions carved into the stones, functions of different structures were shared with me.

On my way towards the Isla de Mujeres, I had to go through Merida even though I had not planned to visit there. I arrived on the second-class bus close to the center of town. The city was big, beautiful, and colorful, like most tourist towns. I stopped in a few hotels and restaurants, and just as I was told, Merida was more expensive than I could afford. Finding a single room to rent was more difficult than in other towns. Tourists were everywhere, dressed in resort clothing and carrying large bags stuffed with purchases from the market, colorful crafts and clothing, designed specifically for tourists.

At the market, a rude American tourist was trying to buy a blanket from a vendor who did not speak English. The American seemed to think that the louder he spoke, the more likely the vendor would understand him, so the American was shouting at a small Mayan man who was trying his best to accommodate the tourist to make a sale.

Interrupting the rude gringo to protect the vendor from more abuse, I yelled, "What are you doing?"

The man looked at me and said, "I'm just trying to make a deal and buy a blanket."

I said, "Why don't you calm down, treat this man with some respect, or get the hell out of here."

He gave me a dirty look and moved on. I apologized to the vendor for the man's behavior. This was not the first time I'd witnessed a gringo without manners, and their behavior embarrassed me as was an American. So even though Merida is a beautiful city, I knew that big tourist towns like that were not for me.

Next, I caught a bus to Chichen Itza, the largest anthropological site of Mayan civilization in the Americas. On the bus I met a couple of English chaps, Kirk and Bill who had come all the way from Britain. We talked about how much fun it would be to spend the night on the top of El Castillo, the tall pyramid with ninety steps to the top. The three of us liked the idea of staying for several days and were surprised that we hadn't crossed paths while visiting many of the same places. We arrived in Piste, a small town outside of Chichen Itza, still about a half hour from our destination. The bus dropped us off at the market to gather supplies, mainly food and liquids. The market had an assortment of *suminisytos de cocina* or kitchen items. I spotted a small sheet-metal alcohol stove, a simple little cooking device that used denatured alcohol, also known as white gas. Kirk and Bill were in the habit of eating *campo*, outside in a field. We bought the stove, beans, tortillas, a can of sweetened condensed milk, *galletas* or cookies and *tepache*, a water replacement sold in the market and on the street. Tepache is a pre-Hispanic fermented beverage made from many ingredients, depending what area of Mexico you are in, but its base is roasted corn and water. In the Northern states, they add chile with prickly pears from the cactus plant and maybe some pineapple. In the Southern states, fresh fruits, flowers, and sugar or honey were added. We also bought some cheap tequila and Kirk had a supply of marijuana.

Chichen Itza turned out to be a remarkable site of seventy or more acres. In the center is El Castillo, a pyramid, and other buildings scattered around the temple grounds. Archeologists and anthropologists from all over the world were present, still studying the site. We were allowed to climb around and move freely on the site; only in 1972 did the site became protected, and not until 2016, did UNESCO declare it one of the Seven Wonders of the World.

Late in the afternoon, we climbed the 91 steps to the top of El Castillo, broke out our sleeping bags and made camp. Later that night, sitting on top of El Castillo, stoned on pot, I gazed up at the stars wondering what this place would have been like in 1500 AD, with 50,000 Mayan Indians occupying the square in the city below. Kirk, Bill and I shared and discussed the brief history we knew of Chichen Itza. Then we fired up the alcohol stove, cooked our warm meal and drank some tequila.

Early the next morning, we started up the stove again, cooked some scrambled eggs and tortillas, drank our tepache, and spent the rest of the day exploring and talking to the men and women working on the site. I remember hanging out with a few archaeologists deciphering the hieroglyphics on the stones. In the evening, I met up with Kirk and Bill and we spent another night at the temple. After almost everyone else had left, a night watchman approached us. His job was to look out for the equipment the archeologists left on site. We offered him a drink of tepache with a tequila chaser, and he saw no reason to prevent us from sleeping on top of the temple. That night, Bill approached me with a concerned look on his face, asking if I was ok. I knew what he was about to say. Something weird had happened he said, I was ready to listen. Kirk joined us. Bill explained that when we were talking earlier my face trembled and I stopped engaging in the conversation and wandered off, not responding to anything they said. They were concerned about me.

I felt exposed. My secret was no longer a secret. I trusted Kirk and Bill, so I was straight with them. I explained that I had seizures, never knew when I was seizing and there was nothing, I could do about it. They expressed concern that I would wander off and hurt myself, but I assured them, that somehow my mind protected me from doing anything harmful to myself. I told them of a time I was riding my bike down a busy street, pulled off the street, had a seizure, and several minutes later I got back on my bike and kept riding. My explanation made them feel more comfortable They accepted my account, and I thanked them for their concern. I was just trying to be a normal person and accept who I was.

The next morning, before Kirk and Bill said goodbye, I thanked them again for their concern. Then I stayed around and checked out a few more things at Chichen Itza. I discovered that they were dredging one of the sacred cenotes, a large sinkhole where human sacrifices took place. The dredging was taking place in a closed-off area away from any tourists. Dredging of the cenotes has been taking place since 1904 using divers. They used large vacuums to suck up fragments of bones, gold, and stone artifacts that had been left behind and were buried deep in rock crevices at the bottom. The guard, who knew we'd camped out on top of El Castillo, ignored me as I mixed in with the dredging team. I stayed long enough to witness the sucking up of small skulls and bone fragments from men, women, and children sacrificed to Mayan gods over 1200 years ago. The dredge, with its long eight-inch diameter tubes, emptied onto large, screened tables where archeologists sifted through the artifacts and human bones.

The next day, I took the second-class bus back to Piste. Arriving at the dock for the ferry to Islas de Mujeres, I had no problem buying a ticket. The boat ride over to the island took no longer than an hour. Crystal-clear water provided a clear view of the sea bottom. The boat carried ten to twenty passengers, mostly fishermen and families, with food and supplies. When we reached the boat dock, I saw a small town with a few buildings, a small market, and one or two little motels. Looking forward to collapsing on the white sandy beach and soaking up some sun, I ventured out to the beach, walking past several fishing huts where you could eat lunch.

The beach was covered with sand dunes I could lie back against and look out over the ocean. It was a perfect setting, bright sun, a little shade from the sand dunes and a view of the water. A brief nap on the beach restored me, and when I woke up, something caught my eye. I thought nothing of it at first, though I was sure something had run past me and over a dune twenty to thirty feet away, but now I looked out and only saw the white sand of the beach. No people, no cars, nothing. So, I let it pass, grabbed a book, sat back, and read. Again, I saw something, low to the ground and hurrying. I sat up and scanned the beach and tree line. It was then

I saw a giant iguana, four feet long, two feet tall with a long tail. It was greenish, with a weird head. I could see the resemblance to the small Iguanas we had as pets when I was a kid, but I had never heard of an iguana large enough to eat a person. I didn't start worrying about being attacked until I noticed three or four more crossing over the vegetated sand dunes. Unable to sit back down and relax, I walked down the beach, passing four or five families and many fishermen. I was excited to see people and talk about the Isle. Of course, I started the conversation about the legato (lizard). Everyone laughed and asked if I was scared. When I admitted I was a little scared, they reassured me and said not to worry, iguanas would not eat me, but they would eat my food if left it unprotected.

It never took long for Mexican families to show their hospitality and offer food or drink, and these folks offered me a bowl of fresh ceviche with a squeeze of lime.

Talking with the locals, I learned that the island had experienced a powerful hurricane (Gilbert) the year before which caused minor damage to the ancient Mayan structures. I enjoyed conversing with one of the mothers who seemed to know the history of the island better than the others. She told stories of slave traders who had settled on the island. One famous trader built a large and beautiful hacienda that was still standing, both the gardens and home. The woman described how when fresh water was piped in, how many more people came to visit the island, and she now worried that if more streets and hotels were built the island would become more like the nearby tourist attraction of Cancun.

Chapter 12

Finally Heading to Sitala

Four days on the Isla De Mujeres meets all my expectations: crystal clear water, white sandy beaches, Mayan ruins, and giant lizards. Working with fishermen and getting paid for helping to pull three-hundred-pound tortoises to shore put a few extra pesos in my pocket. A small boat brought me back to the mainland and Puerto Juarez. Not showering for a week in the belief that cleaning up in the ocean was sufficient was incorrect. I'm clean but carry a thick crust of salt over my body and hair. My skin feels itchy and uncomfortable. I need to rent a cheap hotel room, shower with soap and water, and have my clothes cleaned. Puerto Juarez has few amenities, and my clothes are dirty, justifying me to pay someone to clean them. There are no laundromats in southern Mexico. Laundry is done by hand, a service you find by asking around. The hotel manager knows where to find laundry service, and is a bit stunned to have a young white boy ask for laundry service like a local. I had learned to travel light, two pairs of pants, two white shirts, like those worn by Indian working men. My two pairs of socks that are disgusting. I've quit wearing underwear, a garment that is too much trouble for the way I'm travelling. Needing to clean all my clothes, even the ones I am wearing, I gather my clothes and wrap myself in a towel. I had not perfected the towel wrap, and it tended to fall off. I put my belt on over the towel and walk over to the manager's room. I was told my clothes will be ready that night. I lounge in my room, naked, all day waiting. Luckily, I have reading material and maps to study. There is no TV or radio in the room.

Late in the day, I hear a knock at the door. Adjusting my towel, fastening my belt, I open the door. At the door is a woman with a package wrapped in newspaper. She could not have been over four and a half feet tall, with an innocent, sweet smile. She lifts the package high enough for me to reach easily, preventing me from having to bend over. Not knowing the cost of laundry service nor speaking her dialect, I open my wallet and motion for her to take out what I owe her. Shyly, she took out five pesos. The exchange rate at the time was fourteen pesos to the dollar, it came to forty cents. I couldn't do that. I open the package on the table. Each piece of clothing, cleaned, dried, pressed, and meticulously folded. Knowing that to press clothes an iron has to be heated on hot coals, she must have worked hours on this one job. I pull a twenty-peso bill from my wallet and hand it to her, and she backed off, inferring that was too much. I felt so privileged that she did this for me. Leaning forward, I place the bill in a small bag she's carrying and said, "Ma'alob xi, paatik in bin," that is, thank you and safe travel. I don't know if that was her language, but she seemed to know what I said, or at least the spirit of the words.

Studying a map, I find a shortcut that may prevent me having to backtrack to Merida. The hotel manager did not know of this alternate route. She calls to a man from the back to help me. A man comes out, sizes me up, and asks how he could help. I point on the map to where I'm going and ask about this shortcut. He says this is an old dirt and muddy road. There are no buses, only vehicles *dura* or four-wheel-drive and several men to help cut brush and dig you out of the mud. I had helped cars and buses out of the mud before and knew it was something to be avoided. He knew Chiapas and explained to me that Sitala was one of one hundred and nineteen municipalities that made up the state. Sitala is the poorest municipality in Chapais. They only used the road several times a year to transport coffee picked in the Highlands. If I was with my uncle and the International Scout, we may have taken that route, if only for the adventure. He said the quickest and most dependable way in is to fly in from Tuxtla Gutierrez, the capital of Chiapas. Never had I dreamed of flying on a single-engine plane to reach my destination.

Staring at me, he said, "You know you are going to a very remote area?"

The Lacondon jungle surrounded the Sitala province to the South. He suggested not to travel alone. The Lacondon Indians were primitive people that lived and hunted in the rainforest, and they did not like strangers in their jungle. They hunted with bows and arrows and will protect themselves from outsiders. You have long red hair, and you are white. You're different from the people you will meet. Not wanting him to think I was a lost teenager wandering through the jungle. I explained my uncle, a Jesuit priest lived in Sitala, he had notified the mayor that I would be visiting.

He said, "The Tzeltal Indians in Sitala are peaceful people, having an introduction will help."

The only way to Tuxtla Gutierrez was to backtrack up the Yucatan Peninsula going through Chetumal, which was a two-day trip up the peninsula on a secondary highway going through the state of Quintana Roo. Chetumal, a historical city and the gateway to Central America, bordering British Honduras was a coastal town with picturesque beaches, marinas, and boardwalks, with more attractions than many cities. I grabbed all the brochures I could find about Chetumal and found a room. The room was about seven feet by ten feet, with an open bath, a single bed, and a bedside lamp, with one forty-watt bulb not enough to read by. The next day, I visited the cultural museum, with one of the better Mayan exhibits I had visited. The language exhibit went through the many dialects spoken and how the Aztec and Mayan language combined into others. I could have stayed in Chetumal another day, a perfect Caribbean location, a popular spot where many Mexicans vacationed.

From Chetumal, a bus ride to the middle of the Peninsula to Escarega, a city involved in oil production and refineries. The city smelled of oil and gas and was dirty, not a tourist destination. At a small hole in the wall restaurant, I had a meal with a truck driver. He was making a delivery a few hundred miles away in Chable. The truck driver offered me a ride that far. This started one of the most terrifying trips I took in Mexico.

The truck was not a regular semi box truck. I was climbing onto an old oil tanker truck carrying gasoline. The seat was nothing more than exposed springs and a foam cushion. Exposed wiring covered the dashboard, there was a hole in the floor where you could see the road below. The truck was littered with papers, delivery receipts, old food, little pieces of tortilla everywhere. Starting out was not too bad. We drove through town to the main highway. After several minutes, we built up speed. I got nervous when I looked at the speedometer: we were going seventy miles per hour in a forty-foot gas tanker truck. I remained quiet until the conditions worsened. The road narrowed, traffic increased, potholes became more frequent, no guardrails and a deep culvert on the side of the road.

We hit a large pothole, the truck jumped, gas shot out of the top of the holding tank, and the driver lit a cigarette. The cab smelled of gasoline, I was sure we were going to blow-up. I didn't know how to signal to the driver "there's something wrong here." Not wanting to appear young, scared, and about to lose my life, I somehow convinced myself the driver did this all the time, and he's still alive. We'd be okay.

When we reached our destination, a gas station on the outside of town, I was relieved to get out of that truck. When the door opened, I flew out. Forgetting how high up I was sitting, I dropped three feet to the ground, spraining my ankle. Limping, I found the bus station.

Still a long way from Tuxtla Gutierrez, I splurged and took the ADO bus, a comfortable bus with a bathroom, comparable to a Greyhound, to San Cristobal De las Casas. I sat on the bus next to a government official of one of the municipalities in Chiapas, making the trip interesting. He was traveling to the capital for work. He talked about the difficulties in protecting the Mayan milpas and the Lacondon jungle from large outside companies. Pemex and other oil and lumber companies were trying to develop the rainforest. Efforts were being made from various government and outside groups to protect the Mayan people and their culture in Chiapas. He said, "You are fortunate to see Chiapas and places like Sitala at this time. This safe, simple way of life the Mayan Indians are living in the highlands of Chiapas will not last forever."

Anthropological studies were always going on in Chiapas, especially in the Lacandon rainforest and he told me I could expect to meet people from different countries participating in these explorations. His role in government was coordinating these studies from different countries. This conversation I had in 1971, was seven years before the Mexican government declared southern Chiapas and the Lacondon Jungle a protected area, the Montes Azules Biosphere Reserve. The reserve covers over three thousand square miles of tropical rainforest in Mexico and Central America.

The bus stopped several times in small villages where we could stretch and eat. The food at these stops fascinated me with new smells., colors and shapes. Local people were amused, watching as I examined the food. The next day, we arrived at San Cristobal de Las Casas. A colorful town, houses and buildings painted many colors and a large population of Americans. They lived close to one another, isolated from the local community. I had lunch with a couple from Ohio who had been living there for the last three years. They loved it there, but I didn't understand. How could they love the area when they hadn't learned Spanish or discovered their surroundings? They looked at me like I was crazy to travel alone in Mexico. I looked at them like they were crazy for not doing so, just living in their little compound. Anyway, San Cristóbal was a delightful town, with a beautiful market. A place where I could speak English and drink an American beer.

Tuxtla Gutierrez is my next stop. After a short two-hour bus ride, the airport was my next stop. An airport employee told me that the only planes going into Sitala were private single-engine planes, and I had to reserve a flight. He directed me to the other end of the airport. The clerk must have sensed I had little money and said I could either fly with a licensed pilot or an unlicensed pilot. I would save money flying with an unlicensed pilot, so I opted for that. A man in his thirties stepped forward and introduced himself. I told the pilot where I was going, and he asked when I wanted to leave.

"As soon as possible," I said. The pilot said the flight was four-hundred-kilometers and took about five hours. We would have to leave in the morning, and it would cost $1020 pesos. I agreed and said I would meet him there in the morning. We shook hands, and I was off to find a place to stay.

I was nervous, nervous enough to call home. My parents were aware of what I was doing but didn't know when I was getting there. My mom had spoken with Uncle Bill, and he had reassured her that he had written to Marcos, a friend, and the mayor of Sitala, and told him his nephew may be coming. I assured my parents not to worry and that I planned to return home for a visit when I left Chiapas. They asked when that would be. Spending a year or more was the plan. Of course, my mother said that was too long and to come home sooner. My father got on the phone and sounded more concerned with the airplane than me. My dad, a World War II pilot, had to put in his two cents about flying. I again assured mom and dad I would stay in touch by mail when possible. I didn't want the conversation to sound like our last. Even though I knew if I had an accident or I became ill, I could not let them know quickly.

Arriving at the airport early, Jose, the pilot, was already checking the plane and loading medical supplies for Sitala. The plane looked rather old, having cloth wings, and needing paint. The interior was beyond simple, with very few instruments or controls. Ok, *vamos* (let's go) shouted Jose. We took off and started climbing. I was used to climbing fast and reaching flying altitude in minutes. It took us over twenty minutes to do that. We circled in huge loops, climbing, and climbing to reach an altitude of fifteen hundred feet. Below us, a mountainous rainforest. I didn't know what landmarks Jose was using to navigate. Every so often I could see smoke rising from the forest, or a patch where there was a Milpa, a corn and vegetable field. As we flew deeper into the jungle, it became more mountainous with deep canyons. Hot air rose through the canyons, lifting the plane hundreds of feet in a few seconds. The plane bounced around like a lost balloon rising in the sky. The turbulence was frightening, only being secured by my seatbelt. I knew the pilot could feel my discomfort. He kept looking over at me, assuring me everything will be alright, and we had more mountains and canyons to cross. There was nothing I could do but sit tight. We continued on our roller coaster ride in the sky.

The pilot lowered the plane to 1000 feet and asked me to be on the lookout for a waterfall. He said I would see a shiny vertical strip on the side of a mountain. I didn't know the importance of being on the lookout until he told me I was his navigator. Finding the waterfall would give him confidence that we were flying in the right direction. From there, we were only forty minutes away from Sitala and Jose started asking me to look out for other landmarks. Rivers, fields, and paths through the forest, large cutouts in the trees where there are a half a dozen small huts with reed roofs. Below, I saw a group of men working on the side of the mountain; Jose told me they were picking coffee, and shouted, "It is time for Uxoj," the coffee harvest in the highlands and that Uxoj ke', the coffee harvest in the lowlands, has finished. I was getting excited. We could see civilization below. As we continued at a much lower altitude, Jose said we are getting close. Look out for a white building, a church on the right, surrounded by several smaller brown structures and a grass landing strip. I pointed out a grouping of buildings that Jose said was Chilon and a small *binka*, or farming collective of five to twenty families.

We flew over another canyon, and just as we settled

in on the last stretch, we hit another hot air lift. Every time we came down to a lower altitude, a hot air lift pushed the plane back up into the sky. Finally, we were flying low enough not to get caught by the hot air. We stayed low and circled around a small mountain. Below us was Sitala, no bigger than a football field. An old, maybe thousand square foot white mud and plaster church stood in the middle. The next largest building was smaller, maybe six hundred square feet, with a metal roof, used as a clinic and community building. Next to the clinic was the mayor's office. Ten to fifteen small mud and wood, one-room homes. Chickens, turkeys, pigs, and donkeys running around. Several wood sheds for animals and food storage. The landing strip sat off to the side and we approached the landing strip and took off again, circling the landing strip two or three times. As we circled, people started coming out from everywhere to the landing strip. Jose stuck his arm out the window and waved to the crowd. Everyone started picking up small sticks, rocks, children's toys and whatever so we could land. When the landing strip was cleared of debris, we made our final approach and landed.

Part Three

Chapter 13

Arrived in Sitala

Finally, in Sitala, I'm the *sobrino* (nephew) de Padre Nolan, Uncle Bill, and I soon learned Padre Nolan had given me an excellent introduction to the mayor and community. But he'd not prepared them for my unkempt below the shoulder bright red hair, longish red beard, and pale skin. When exiting the plane, some turned their back to me, some ran away, some cried, but most of them just stared.

They were familiar with outsiders, but none that looked like me. Tzeltal Indians are of small stature with olive brown skin color and dark hair; the men all had the same haircut, the one that looks like someone put a bowl on the head and trimmed around it. Men wore traditional white loose-fitting pants and white shirts; the women wore colorful hand embroidered skirts and blouses. The teenagers and children wore cast off American clothing aid agencies had brought. Everyone was barefoot or wore sandals. I smiled and tried to look friendly.

Thankfully, the mayor of Sitala, Marcos, stepped forward and introduced me to everyone. "This is the sobrino of our friend, Padre Nolan. He is going to stay with us for some time." Then, everyone greeted me, eager to meet the sobrino de Padre Nolan.

All I could hear was *bin abijil* (what is your name) and *banti talemat* (where are you from). Marcos stepped in and said to me, "You will have time to meet everyone later. Now we must meet the elders of Sitala."

As I left with Marcos, everyone was saying *ban'che* (safe travel) even though we were only walking several yards through the village.

We walked a short distance to an *atut* (home) of one of the elders, who asked me *no'clan* (sit down). I sat on the dirt floor while Marcos explained to the four men who I was and what I was doing here. The men smiled and nodded their heads. One man poured me water in a small *uk'ap* (a dried squash gourd cut in half into a bowl). I reached over and accepted the *uk'ap* and drank the water. It was evident that the men were upset, with one man leaving. I could see by the way they were speaking to each other that something was not right. Marcos motioned be to come outside, concern showing in his face. I got up and walked out the door. He explained that the water was not to drink. It is used to cleanse one's mouth, expelling evil words that came out of one's mouth. The tradition is to swish the water, then spit it out on the ground. Swallowing the water was like swallowing your own waste.

I asked, "What should I do?"

Marcos said when we entered the room, I was to say to the elders *Ya xaxon bin cum Cutie* (excuse me, I am sorry) and he would do the rest. He then settled the men down by explaining to them it was not my custom to rinse the mouth. This was difficult for them to understand since they knew of no other customs than their own.

With that awkwardness settled, one elder picked up a large gourd, and poured a small amount of a liquid into a sipping size gourd. I took a taste and clenched my face. A clear liquor, a jungle moonshine made from sugar cane. We drank, and visited for a short while, Marcos acting as my interpreter. Marcos's apology must have been effective, because when we left, they all said *ban'che, ban'che* (safe travel).

Marcos said, "Let's get some food" and we went to his home, where he introduced me to his wife, Itotie, which means dance. Although her Spanish was okay, Marcos spoke to her in Tzeltal which she preferred. Carrying on a conversation was challenging without Marcos's help. She welcomed me into her home, introduced me to their two young children and offered me water, *a wabon ja'* (would you like water). It was hard paying attention to a foreign language with the children laughing, playing, and trying to get my attention.

We sat and had a meal together. Squash, beans, and pork cooked together in a ball of cornmeal. A tasty meal, and much less spicy than the traditional Mexican food I'd become accustomed to eating. For dessert we ate *illaqillalla*, a long green pod, which when split open, revealed a flat almond shaped seed, covered in a white fluffy sweet meat. I did my best to copy how the others ate the fruit, sucking on the seed to pull the meat off the seed. An unusual, sweet fruit, unlike anything I'd ever had before.

Afterward, Marcos and I walked around the town and he explained how they used the three buildings next to the church in the middle of town. We stopped by the clinic. People kept coming up to us asking questions I could not answer. Marcos, seeing that I was struggling to speak, suggested I just say *kuxi* (greetings) in Tzeltal. That was a relief. *Kuxi* became my go to word in Tzeltal. As we continued, I saw *tsi'w* (men working with wood). Two men were splitting fence posts. They faced one another while standing on a large log. They each swung their axe in a continuous motion facing each other, one man taking a swing and a step backwards, the other taking a swing and a step forward, axes missing each other's heads by inches. While I watched in amazement, they split this log into six fence posts while risking their lives. We continued to the *milpas* (corn, bean, and vegetable fields). It was the growing season and there were dozens of women and children planting and working in the *milpa*. They tended to the *mayil* (squash), *inkinab* (beans), *ixlm* (corn), *ich chili* (peppers) and other vegetables that I couldn't identify. There are over fifteen words for beans in Tzeltal, among them, a word for when the bean flower appears, a word for when the bean appears, a word for when the bean appears lumpy with seeds. There are different words for yellow, red and brown beans and words for soft, mushy and leathery beans. Almost all words have other words that describe what stage or condition the subject is in. About as far as I got with the Tzeltal language was the simplistic form of the word.

I wandered the *milpa* observing different types of farming. The only metal edged tools I saw being used were machetes, primitive hoes, and axes. Women in the bean field were using the *awv'll* (a wooden pole with a pointed end used to push a small hole in the soil to plant a seed). I asked Marcos how they prepared the fields, as the soil was not cultivated. Marcos explained that they used fire to burn the fields in order to clear away the last year's harvest. They do not cultivate the soil, they use the *awv'll* to plant seeds and a short-handled hoe to cut back unwanted vegetation. The ash from the burning provides for the soil's nourishment. This Mayan method of farming has been used for thousands of years.

After touring the milpa, meeting many people, and drinking sugar cane liquor, I needed to rest. I met Marcos again later in the day to discuss a schedule for what I will be doing in Sitala. I was interested in working in the clinic. This interest may have come from my grandfather, my mother's father being an Admiral and doctor in the Navy. He was stationed in Haiti, responsible for the leprosy care program for all the Caribbean islands for over thirty years. I thought about working with the men and women picking coffee or farming in the milpa. Marcos suggested, I start in the clinic when Abre, the clinic nurse, returned in a few days. He said Abre spoke Spanish and could use my assistance, as well as help me with the Tzeltal language.

The only electricity in Sitala was a small generator in the clinic. The generator was only big enough to power two lights in the clinic, one in the church, and three lights outside the clinic entrance, which also provided partial lighting to the center plaza. The day ended with the sun going down. Homes had candles, small oil lamps and open fires for cooking. The generator only ran when needed.

Marcos showed me the bed that was prepared in my *atut*. The bed resembled a raised garden, the size of a full-sized bed full of pine needles. The pine needles had to be 8 to 10 inches thick, which kept bugs and insects away. I had my dinner at Marcos' house and called it a night. I was given an oil light to use as needed. Without a door on my atut, there was limited privacy. I lay on my back with my head towards the door; adjusting to the pine needle bed was no more difficult than getting used to the straw beds in cheap hotels.

As I lay there thinking about the amazing day I'd had, I sensed someone or something close. It was dark, and as my eyes had not adjusted to the darkness, I distinguished what I thought was a flicker of light, like a candle dancing in the dark. I lay still, a little scared. I could see the candle flame getting closer, then I heard a rustling noise, like the swooshing of a skirt or dress close to me. Not moving, thinking no one is going to hurt me, I had made no enemies. Suddenly, I felt a hair being plucked from my head, then two more. I was about to jump up when the scuffling of skirts moved away from me. When it became quiet again, I raised my body, and turned my head to look behind me. Two short women in black skirts were walking away. They took my bright red hair, and I thought this may have had something to do with local witchcraft. I imagined becoming part of a brujas (witches) altar, or they could have been using my hair to cast a spell on me. I never knew what they did with my hair, but nothing bad seemed to come of it.

In the morning, I was still shaken and confused from the visitation the night before. I hoped not to have any other body parts snatched from me in the night. Breakfast was with one of the elders and his family. It was raining, we ate inside his one room home. His house was different, much more primitive than Marcos's house. There were no cupboards, only ropes hanging from the ceiling. At the end of each rope were cooking utensils and food. At the top of each rope a dried gourd cut in half hung. This was to keep the rodents that lived in the thatched roof from coming into the house. There was a small oil burning stove sitting on a primitive table made of painted sheet metal, balanced on two wooden stumps with an open fire on the dirt floor, used for breads and tortillas.

Children were playing, adults were carrying on with their business. It looked like any normal family, although very different from mine. The ventilation was poor in the *atut* and the air was filled with smoke. Breathing in this air seemed unhealthy and I ate fast, staying for only about ten to fifteen minutes. I was getting light-headed and nauseated and rushed my visit, so I could get back into the fresh air. I said *bon'che* (see you later) and left, taking some deep breaths when leaving and went to my atut for a few minutes to recoup.

Later that day I heard music and followed it to the center of town, near the church. There was a guitar, a primitive violin, a bamboo flute, a rattle and a man with a blade of grass tucked between his upper lip and nose, whose music sounding like a kazoo. The music was upbeat, I felt like moving. People gathered to *a'kot* (dance), people dance standing in rows, moving several steps forward and several steps backward, or just shifting their bodies side to side, their arms flapping like birds. Getting up, I took part in the dance, doing my best to imitate their movements. They did not dance as couples, but as a group. The Mayan people are shy and respectful of others. This social dancing is done slowly not holding on to each other.

Later I went to another of the elder's houses to eat dessert. This was fresh fruit, smothered in *chap* (honey). I asked if they have bee hives; he said yes, outside the door. After we ate, we went outside and he pointed to a small *ta'yejil* (beehive) no bigger than a small bird house, mounted on the outside wall. He said all the homes have one. If you were going to be a bee, the rainforest of southern Chiapas is where you would want to live. Abundant blossoms from thousands of coffee tree flowers and milpas blooming throughout the year. A beehive on every home is so practical and an environmental solution to bee's disappearing.

Working in the milpa was tough. The Tzeltal Indian body seemed adapted for squatting and working for hours. My six foot, one-hundred-and-seventy-pound body was too big for squatting in the tropical sun for hours. The workers kept saying *jayeb awabilal* (how do you feel), seeing how awkward I looked with tight jeans jabbing a pointed pole in the ground and a handful of corn seeds in the other, squatting and moving down a row of corn trying to work as they were. The Indian women planted ten seeds to every one of my seeds. Marcos walked over, patted me on the back saying they have had a lot of practice. I returned the following day not wanting to be seen as a quitter.

The next day, I spent helping a man sharpen machetes and *jstor* (hoes). The *ma'ak kuja'ik* (man who sharpens blades) had with three large, flat stones he carried on his back. Each stone was about eight inches wide by eighteen inches long and two inches thick each having a different grit for different stages of sharpening. The stones were passed down to him through generations. Sharpening was his contribution to working in the milpa. Language was not a problem; sharpening was all hands-on learning. He gently showed me how he sharpened using his sharpening stones. Being a woodworker most of my life, I still use the correct pressure, angles, and body position he taught me.

That evening at dinner with Marcos and his family, we ate spider monkey. Spider monkey is considered a bush meat and commonly eaten in Southern Mexico as a special dish. Spider monkey is a white meat and tastes like juicy pork. The meat was cut up in small cubes and served with squash, beans and a selection of peppers. I preferred the roasted ribs. Not too spicy, the Mayan way.

We talked about my blade sharpening experiences in the milpa. Marcos said sharp tools can be used as weapons so only men do this job, a woman's main purpose was to love and comfort, and did not go into battle. The word battle started a conversation about conflicts between Indians in the rainforest. I've never forgotten the wisdom of Marcos' explanation. "The people in the rainforest and Lacandon jungle do not have wars, only conflicts. Conflicts can be resolved; wars leave bad lasting memories. Although the

Lacandon people have gotten very close to what we consider war. Their aggressive and warlike attitude is why people in the highlands or lowlands do not intermingle with the Lacandon people."

The Lacandon people are a tiny population, maybe eight to nine hundred people. Living off the land in the jungle, all their food comes from within the jungle and forest, and they hunt and fight with bows and arrows. Marcos went into a small storage shed and returned with a bow and arrow from the Lacandon people to share with me. He said one conflict we have with the Lacandon is that they make their bows from the sip che' tree. Tzeltal's' consider this tree sacred and a spirit of our forest. I asked about the trees in the surrounding forest. Marcos said, "I will be told, but not now, it was getting late."

Before I left, I was told Abre, the *chu'untes* (nurse), should be back in the morning, and we agreed to meet at the clinic.

Chapter 14

The Clinic

In the morning, I meet Abre, an attractive woman in her thirties. College educated, and a Spanish speaker, she is quiet, but not shy in her behavior. Abre is of Mayan descent, born in Sitala, and returning after training as a nurse. Abre is the *chu'untes* (nurse) and as close as one can be to a *jtopoxtawan* (doctor) at the clinic.

The clinic is approximately seven-hundred square feet, with cubical shelving along two walls where sample medicines are kept. An enormous book, the pharmacological pill dictionary, sits on a wooden table. Medicine samples provided by either the government or medical aid agencies are regularly delivered to the clinic, wrapped in bubble wrap, transported on planes like the one I arrived on. Abre and I went over the procedure for sorting medicines, using the book to identify each pill by name and use. There are antibiotics, antihistamines, pain medicines, anti-diarrheal and steroids. The clinic was well supplied with medicines and first aid type supplies. My job will be to sort sample medicines and store them correctly, as well as helping as needed.

In a normal day at the clinic we saw entire families, mothers with children, and people who had been injured in accidents. Abre checked in patients and kept records, not just their health records, but also of where they lived, any deaths or new members in the family. She kept track of children attending school in all 114 localities in the municipality of Sitala. These localities are called *bin'kas*. A *bin'ka* is like a small village with anywhere from five to twenty families living in a communal setting.

Schools are scattered throughout the localities, in homes or separate buildings. Usually the buildings were wood plank, or mud with sheet metal or thatched roofs and dirt floors. Schools taught classes in Mayan culture, Mayan spirits, celebrations, Spanish, and simple math. Classes identifying local plants and animals, manners, personal health, working in the *milpa* and coffee gathering were taught. Abre encouraged me to learn the Tzeltal language, which is very complex. Verbs are not one word, but a full phrase describing an action. It is a tiny language that only deals with what surrounds a twenty-five-mile radius.

My use of Tzeltal improved working at the clinic. Abre wrote a list of phrases to learn. *Binora xtalat* (where are you coming from?), *bin abijil* (what is your name?), *banti ayte chamel* (where are you sick?), *bin yilel sucub awu'un* (how do you feel?), *ay bal wayel* (did you sleep well?), *ay bal awinal* (are you hungry?). The more I learned, the more phrases were given to me to work with. A privacy curtain divided the public part of the clinic from the treatment area, which has a treatment room with a raised wooden exam table covered by a cushion made of stacked cloth with a cover sheet. It seemed like a maternity clinic, wound clinic, pediatric clinic, all in one. People traveled to the clinic by foot, sometimes as far as three or four miles, or even further. While Abre was attending to patients, I would provide the people waiting with water and food after their travels. Many came in with emergencies and we'd have to help them fast. If Abre was in the middle of helping someone else, I would shout out the emergency and she would shout back, giving me instructions on what to do next. Put pressure on the wound, clean them up, get them a glass of water, give them an aspirin, find a pillow, and lay them down with their head raised. As time went on, Abre gave me more responsibility. She took over big emergencies, and I helped with women giving birth, acting almost as a doula, standing by the women in delivery, encouraging them to *laktz'un* (push). Outside, the clinic had a birthing pole planted in the ground that women could hold on to as they squatted to deliver their babies. Women whose mothers had delivered using a birthing pole were more inclined to deliver by this means. When women used the birthing pole, my job was to bring out the supplies or sometimes just waiting with a nervous new father. We delivered more than five babies each month.

Vaccinations were an important part of our service. Getting vaccines was not popular. Sticking people with a needle was unheard of in Mayan culture. Abre explained that the closest word to giving an injection in Tzeltal was to be *ts'up* (stab). Not very inviting, and there were few takers without a lot of education first. Abre educated mothers on the importance of the vaccines, and she could often get the message across by explaining the history of smallpox and how it killed over 50 percent of their population years before. Some would take the vaccine, and some would not.

One of the major accomplishments of the Mayan empire was medicine. The Mayan rainforest has provided many, if not most, of the plants and herbs still used in medicines today. The Mayan people had been using these plants and herbs for thousands of years before pharmacological science started putting these them into a pill form. As in ancient Chinese medicine and Ayurvedic medicine in India, ancient Mayan medicine was based on the balance of the body and the soul. People believed that there was no separation between the spirit and the body. Abre was a wealth of knowledge of ancient and today's Mayan medicine. I like to compare Mayan medicine to seeing an herbalist, spiritualists, priest, witch, surgeon, and doctor all in one. Herbs were cooked and inhaled, applied, rubbed and made into enemas. Shamans performed rituals for cleansing, fasting, and sweating. Sweating was like the sweating ceremonies used by American Indians. They used sweat baths in Mayan medicine for centuries. *Dzac yahes*, the Mayan herbalists, were highly respected and were often visited prior to coming to the clinic.

After several weeks had passed, I began to feel guilty for not telling Abre about my seizures. I had a responsibility to let Abre know my medical history, what if I had a seizure, while I was working at the clinic? Abre would either accept me as I was or tell me I couldn't work in the clinic. Abre may have already known about the seizures, through Marcos, but I needed to have the conversation with her myself. Abre said she had seen me have seizures, and that I was having *ochlo'haxoh* (fits), the word describes involuntary body movements. In Mayan culture, having seizures related to those being possessed by spirits through the power of demons. People with epilepsy seizures struggled between the armadillo and the human spirit. The struggle was because the armadillo was seeking revenge for being hunted.

She said that the seizures I had when I walked around were not violent convulsions and could be considered dancing with the spirits. Any type of *ochlo'haxoh* is considered a supernatural gift and not as an illness. I told her I was almost out of medicine, she said she would get it for me. A runner came through once every two or three weeks and she would have them include the medicine in the next airdrop and not to worry. She promised to monitor me. I asked if I should stay away from the clinic; she said, of course not. I was relieved she did not see me as weird, different, or a liability.

A few weeks later, a teen-age boy came into the clinic with his mother, crying and bent over in pain. His mother was crying. I asked *bank'uxul* (where does it hurt?) and he pointed to his belly button and the right side of the stomach below the ribs. I called back to Abre, who was behind the curtain with another patient. She asked where he was from, and he said Tulaquil, five miles away. She told me she would be there in a minute, and I was to take his temperature, make him comfortable and get his mother some water. Quickly, the boy's pain worsened, and he vomited. Abre heard him crying out in excruciating pain. She ushered her other patient out so we could get the young man on the table. His fever was high, and he had chills. Abre said he had appendicitis. She asked me to get the hefty anatomy book off the shelf. She flipped to the page she wanted saying she had assisted as a nurse in an appendix's removal, but never done it by herself. Saying there was no time to waste, she asked me to get all the antibiotics we had together. She grabbed what else she needed, handing me two sample packages of antibiotics to give to the boy. We were preparing to operate.

Abre bustled around, preparing a clean surgical area behind the curtain. We were going to operate in this small building with a dirt floor and only a generator for lights and I was going to assist. There was a complete surgical package in a cardboard box in the back of the clinic. This boy had been walking for over six hours to reach the clinic, and an infected appendix can burst at any time. We had to move quickly.

"Let's get started," she shouted nervously.

My job was to hold up the anatomy book while she operated. We had no general anesthesia, only old-fashioned ether. Abre folded a gauze pad placed it over the boy's mouth and dripped the ether over the gauze. When the boy was asleep, she took his blood pressure and pulse. With a pen, she marked out the incision she was ready to make. She was sweating. I grabbed another gauze pad and wiped her forehead.

She looked up and said, "Thanks."

This would be one of my jobs.

An incision, four inches long, just big enough for her small hands was made. I controlled the bleeding, using gauze pads, so Abre could see. Abre looked at the anatomy book as she moved his intestines around in order to reach the appendix. She was careful not to break the appendix open or the infection could spread throughout his abdomen. Lifting the boy's eyelid, she could tell if he was still asleep. She carefully pulled the long stringy intestine up close to the skin and asked me to put down the book and hold the incision open. Grabbing a pair of scissors, Abre cut the swollen appendix off at the wall of his colon. I almost fainted seeing what she had done, but with a big smile Abre lifted out the infected appendix. Abre took the boy's blood pressure again then closed the wound on the colon and closed the incision, while I sat by the mother offering her water and a piece of fruit. Later, Abre prepared a place for the mother to lie down. Several women came to the clinic with food, drink, and dry herbs to burn. When the women left, several men arrived at the clinic to play music. Marcos also came by and said the music they were playing was for healing and comfort. Abre spent the entire night with the mother and her son. She used this time to explain all that they needed to know to care for him while he recovered from the surgery. Before I left. I checked in with Abre and told her she was not only a *chu'untes* (nurse); she was a *jpost awana* (doctor). She thanked me for the help and said she would see me in the morning. In Tzeltal she said, *wayalat ba ta lec* (sleep well).

The next morning, refreshed after a good night's sleep, I headed over to the clinic, where women were holding baskets of food for Abre, the boy and his mother. I was approached by another woman who offered me food, saying *Abokoluk, Abokoluk* (thank you, thank you). The villagers depend on each other for everything. Everyone has their own role to play in the community, whether it is working in the milpa, cooking, sharpening blades, bringing food to a nurse, or being the nurse. Everybody is appreciated for their contribution.

Days turned into weeks; weeks turned to months, and before I knew it almost a year had passed. Playing frisbee in the center of town with the *ch'inil* (children). Sorting samples at the clinic and talking with Marcos and Abre about what was going on in other parts of Mexico. Both worried about the student revolution in Mexico City and how the workers' revolution was finding its way to Chiapas. The health of the Tzeltal, Lacondon, and Chuj people was in jeopardy. People from the oil and cattle industries were coming into the rainforest and spreading new illnesses and viruses that the people in the rainforest were not immune to.

One morning, I had my first contact with people outside the rainforest visiting Sitala and surrounding localities. Two men, and a young woman, along with their helpers were walking towards the center of town. Marcos came out of his one room office to greet our visitors. I felt so important when, in Spanish, Marcos introduced me to them. Their native language was French, which was no good to either Marcos or me. We were thankful that they also spoke Spanish, although with a French accent. They were associated with an organization similar to our Peace Corps that worked in Public Health worldwide. Their welcome, like mine, required meeting the elders and explaining their purpose for being in the area. I discovered this was not so much an interrogation, but more of the elders being nosy. They had traveled from Bachajon, twenty miles away.

Their message was centered around public health. They talked to people about keeping their chickens out of the houses and especially off the tables where they ate. Their other message was to encourage people to raise more pigs and fewer turkeys. They explained that a turkey eats more than a pig and meat from a pig provides more protein than a turkey. Turkeys are picky eaters and ate corn and other grains which were staples to the Indian diet. If the corn they grew to feed turkeys was used for fuel and cooking oil their quality of life could improve substantially. Turkeys are known to have depleted corn and other grains in many areas. Pigs are not picky; they even eat human waste. The French visitors also spread the word about better hygiene, washing hands, brushing teeth and different ways to store and preserve food. Much of what they were teaching was to prevent *ekojol* (diarrhea) which is one of the biggest contributors to childhood death in the world. They taught mothers not to let their children nibble on unripe fruit, which led to diarrhea. They also advised that children eating sugar cane all day is a major cause of tooth decay. Dental care is not available in the forest, which was regretfully obvious. The ancient Mayans were skilled in dental care, filling cavities, installing crowns, and making dentures from animal bones. This skill was lost somewhere in their history and never replaced. The French left small graphic posters showing hand washing, brushing teeth, and keeping chickens out of the house. After three days they left, leaving a supply of toothbrushes and toothpaste. I came to understand what they were saying about turkeys. Turkeys ravish the seed and grain and scorch the fields wherever they go. Marcos could see the benefits of making fuel from corn. Fuel for the generator is brought in on the backs of men and animals over long distances.

On March nineteenth, Saint Joseph Day, it was a day of celebration, a time of music and eating with others. Women in the localities brought food to the center of Sitala. They set up crude tables for food and drink. The women, men and children dressed up in their best hand embroidered traditional black skirts and blouses, men in white pants and shirts. Several men carried large slit drums and guitars. There were flutes and colorful flags. Everyone lined up in single file and walked to the atut of the mayor. With no televisions, radios, books, or magazines, their only entertainment is talking and telling stories. When the procession came to a home, they would proceed with a lengthy introduction. One man would start talking about the procession from last year, naming everyone who'd participated. After the names of the families and the names of the music played, the musicians would start playing. Then the gratitude began, thanking everyone who'd opened their home for the procession the year before. We must have visited a dozen or more homes, repeating the same thing at each one. I was not bored but exhausted from moving at a pace slower than a snail. We circled back to the center of town in front of the church and continued the celebration, eating, drinking, and listening to music for the rest of the day.

During the celebration, children were acting like children anywhere, playing around except for a few teenage boys. I spotted a group of boys beneath a tree showing off their sling shot skills. They were expert shots. They could shoot the narrow stems of the Mango fruit and catch the fruit before it hit the ground, the younger children jumping around asking for the fruit that had fallen. Back at the tables, everyone was eating and enjoying themselves. A few men had too much to drink and were acting drunk and just like here in the states their wives came to usher them home.

A pig was brought to the party to be slaughtered. A designated elderly man was offered a long, thin, three-foot knife. He stood in one place while the pig was brought up next to him. Two men came forward to position the pig's neck to be stabbed. The older man took the long knife, studied the pig. Then accurately pushed the knife into the pig's neck. The rear legs of the pig were tied and hung to bleed. A fire pit had been prepared for the pig to cook overnight. The next morning, they butchered the pig, and handed out the meat to whoever was there.

A week later, two men were talking, telling stories, and drinking under a tree on the outskirts of town. One man started talking about the other man's wife. They got into a fight, and one man picked up a machete, started swinging and hit the other man multiple times. The badly cut up man was found on a path. Abre was notified and brought him back to the clinic with help. After evaluating the situation, Abre sent for me. I was at the milpa, sharpening blades. I came quickly, knowing something big must be happening.

When I entered the clinic, I was shocked. What happened? Abre said, "There is too much work here for one person. I need you to help me stitch him up."

Never having sewn a wound before, I did not know what to think. Abre looked at me and said, "You will soon be an expert, *awocalluc coltayabon* (help me, please)."

She explained the cuts were flesh wounds, not deep and that's why the bleeding wasn't too bad. If he had been cut deeper, into veins and arteries, he may have already bled to death. Abre asked if I remembered the word, *lo'kchichel* (bleeding). The man was put to sleep with ether. She showed to me how to tie a stitch. I thought it would be like sewing, one continuous thread, but I was mistaken. Each stitch is an individual *p'ok* (knot).

When we were done, the two of us had tied 128 stitches. While collecting the dressing and bandages Abre, sent for *chichim* (older wise women), who prepared an ointment from plants in the forest for healing and pain. She said ancient Mayan medicine sometimes works better than anything she has ever used.

I had not seen this man, Uton, for several months and asked Marcos how he was doing. Marcos said he was badly scarred, and he rarely came out in public because he scared the children. Uton lived in a small atut on the outskirts of town. I found him in the milpa one day. The poor man's wounds were only months old, and the scars were swollen, purple, and horrifying. He had lost an eye and one of his ears. Many of his scars turned thick and raised off his skin. I approached and greeted him bin awilel (how are you). He knew I was with Abre in the clinic when he arrived for help. Uton looked up at me, brought his hands up to his face and just cried. I said *bin cum cute* (I'm sorry) and walked away. I went to the clinic and told Abre that I visited Uton. Abre told me that his mental scars are worse than his physical scars. I felt terrible for Uton but also glad I helped with the stitching even though I was partially responsible for the scarring on his face, body, and mind.

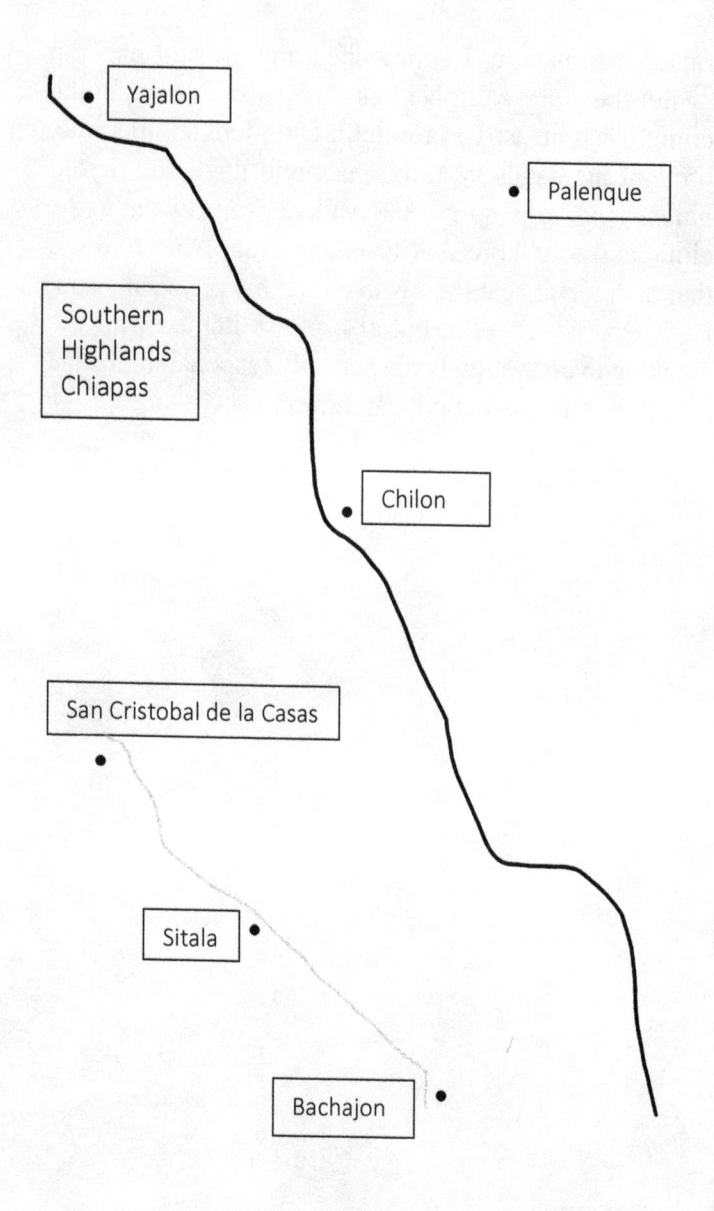

- Yajalon
- Palenque
- Southern Highlands Chiapas
- Chilon
- San Cristobal de la Casas
- Sitala
- Bachajon

Chapter 15

Yajalon, Bachajon and Chilon

The end of *ha'al* (rainy season), was near, January being the wettest month of the year. If traveling by foot, it's best to travel after January. Not that it does not rain in the other months; it rains a little every day of the year. Abre and Marcos invited me to meet and discuss their upcoming plans to travel to the municipalities of Yajalon, Bachajon, and Chilon, all adjacent municipalities to Sitala. They are going to be traveling with a Jesuit priest and a doctor. They plan to be gone at least three to four months. We will have to be back for *kopje* (coffee picking) season. Marcos said we would travel on *chej* (mule) with *six j' a' tel (h*elpers), who *kuch ta patel* (traveling on foot) and donkeys carrying the bulk of our supplies.

I ask what the purpose of the trip is and Abre spoke up and said they try to make the trip every year to visit their neighbors. They rarely go until after coffee season, but they had heard there are problems with *ekojol* (diarrhea) in the area. Padre A (I am going to use the name Padre "A" for his privacy), was flying in with Dr. Canhu, a doctor from San Cristobal, part of a group of doctors who travel to the highlands bi-annually to care for the people. He will bring with him medicines and IV liquids for dehydration. Many people have *laj* (died) and Padre A wants to perform funerals for the families.

Ever since the Spanish invasion of 1500s, the Catholic church has played an important part in protecting the indigenous population throughout Mexico, including the Indians living in the rainforest bordering Guatemala. Over the last one to two hundred years, Catholic priests have protected the people, and the rainforest, from cattle farmers, loggers, oil, and mining interests. Priests have proselytized for the Catholic church and shared their beliefs in strange ways. For instance, Catholics say Jesus was crucified and later met his father in heaven. Mayans say Jesus was *ch'olan* (sacrificed) and offered to the upper world. Mayan culture looks at saints as if they are demons or spirts from the underworld waiting to go to the upper world. Catholic brothers brought the idea of the devil which became the focus of witchcraft. Mayan Indians believe in saints the same way they think of animal spirits. The Mayan people only understand Catholicism when associated with Mayan beliefs of spirits, demons, astrology, animals, earth's energy points and non-human creatures they share with the earth.

Before we leave, I need to acquire transportation for the trip, an older *Chek* (mule) was available, a sturdy animal who had been on this trip before. I bought the mule knowing I could sell her back when I returned. This mule is the same mule my Uncle Bill rode when he took this same trip years earlier. This feels like a good omen. The mule had a noble name, *Muk'ul Dak* (Big Daddy). He was huge, and difficult to mount because he was so *chek'an* (tall). I was given a set of *koxtal* (a type of saddle bag) to carry my things plus whatever would fit from the clinic. We met every day for over a week, gathering supplies, packing the animals and getting ready. Marcos spent time finishing work pertaining to governing Sitala.

Finally, we are all ready, and awaiting Padre A's and Dr. Canhu's arrival. Mules are waiting for them, already packed with the supplies needed to say Mass and to prepare for funerals. Our *j'a' tel,* the six men traveling with us, have two donkeys fully packed. The next morning, we leave on a narrow mountainous path, muddy, and overgrown. It was raining when we left, and we had no umbrellas. Three of the six men stayed ahead of us, keeping the path clear from fallen trees and thick brush. These men found large ferns, each frond two to three feet wide and brought them to us to use as umbrellas. The wide fern worked just as well as any umbrella. While working, the *j'a' tel* also hunted for food to bring as gifts, into the small local villages and towns we were visiting. One day along the trail, we met up with the *j'a' tel*. They had been waiting for us on the trail to show us a huge seven-foot Boa Constrictor up in a tree. They wanted to check with Marcos and ask if the snake was too big to bring with us. It must have been five inches in diameter and weighed two to three hundred pounds, and Marcos nodded to bring the snake. The Boa had wrapped itself around several tree limbs. The men knew that before the snake tightened all its muscles, they had to break it's back. They found a medium-sized log about 2" in diameter and about five feet long. A man took the log over to the tree, and, swinging hard, he struck the back of the snake. Another man stared closely at the snake and yelled out *lek' lek'* (good, good). We left the snake alone to relax its grip before untangling it from the tree.

A lot of conversation went on between the Tzeltal men. I could tell by their body language they were discussing something serious. I asked Marcos what they were saying. Marcos explained the Mayan culture had deep beliefs how animals, humans and the environment balance one another. Snakes play an important role in creating this balance. The men were discussing how we could thank the snake for the sacrifice it made giving us food. The men determined that to create a balance; we needed to ensure that after the body of the snake was removed, there was no sign of death left in the jungle for other snakes to find. This would make the environment clean for the other snakes to live. The men started a fire to have a burning ritual, and the log used to kill the snake was went in the blaze. This fire energy would spread the smoke and ash into the world so it could never come back together to form another log to kill another snake. After the ritual, they loaded the snake onto one of the pack animals and we left. Bachajon was another ten miles away. It rained and again a man ran out into the forest and gathered ferns for us to use as umbrellas.

My mule, *Muk'ul dak*, she had a smooth gait and an easy-going demeanor. It surprised me how quickly we attached to each other. The only time we had a problem was when we came upon *ajch'al* (mud) deeper than four inches. I don't know how the mule knew how deep the mud was, but she did. Muk'ul dak refused to cross mud deeper than four inches. Three inches was fine, four inches of mud was a stubborn no. Muk'ul dak would just stop and refuse to move. Mules have a way about them. There is no way to convince them to do something they do not want to do. She would walk a mile or more to get around deep mud. Everyone knew about her mud issue as they had traveled with her before. Whenever we came to mud on the trail, all the others in our group crossed the mud and keep going down the path, knowing we would catch up after Muk'ul dak found a way around the mud. Soon she would find a mud less route, circle back and rejoin the group. Mules are gregarious animals; they like to be around one another, and she tried very hard to find her way back to the others as quickly as possible. Mules typically keep a steady pace, never too fast, never too slow. When we got within eyesight of our group, Muk'ul dak was so eager to catch up, she would start to trot. The men walking in front of us turned around and *liy* (laugh) at the sight of a huge, impatient mule in a hurry, trying to catch up with the group.

Whenever hungry, we would stop to *ochan* (eat). I'd pull out my *uk'ap*. They handed me a handful of *uc'ohmac'il* (ground corn with a little sugar) to be mixed with water. Following by example, I ate with two fingers. One man ran off into the forest and within a couple of minutes came back with a selection of fresh fruits to eat. There are over sixty edible fruits in the forest. I don't always know what fruit I'm eating, but it's always good.

After a thirteen-hour trip on a mule, I was grateful when we finally arrived. Bachajon was one of the larger municipalities of the rainforest and it had road access to San Cristobal, although it was a dirt road, passable only at certain times of the year. Sitala, where we had come from, was the smallest municipality in the rain forest and was the most deprived and the poorest. Even though Bachajon did not have electricity, nor running water, the village had several generators providing lights several hours per day. Entering Bachajon felt like a trip to the city. The elders greeted us with the welcoming *bin awilel* (how was your travel). When they looked at me, I had to go through the *banti talemat* (where are you from) routine. When I told them I was from the United States they looked at me strangely and said *pues?* Which meant "I don't understand." They did not know of the United States. Then, the next question, *bin abijil* (what is your name). I replied *Jxum* (John). The name John, which is not a Tzeltal name is a phonetic pronunciation for Saint John in the Bible. After the introduction process, we went to the *opisyal's* (mayor) office. I knew what would happen and would not embarrass myself. Entering the home, I saw primitive wooden chairs placed in a circle. We each stood behind our chair, and someone said *huk* (sit). First, we had to cleanse our mouths. The *ch'op* (water jug or gourd) was passed around, and this time I knew the process. I took a small sip, swished it in my mouth and spit on the dirt floor. We sat and the *e'xec* (group drink) was offered. In Bachajon, many more people spoke Spanish, which was helpful, but even so, Abre set me up with a young man named *Ma'k,* who helped me to follow the discussion about the health of the community, which was spoken in three or four dialects. The doctor talked about *ekojol* (diarrhea), *k'ajk* (fever) and *obal* (cough). Dr. Canhu and Abre both spoke about the importance of cleanliness to prevent diseases such as diarrhea. They expressed the importance of cleaning hands and keeping animals away from the kitchens. The villages that were hardest hit with illness were those further away from the center of town. A schedule for visiting each of the more remote villages was developed. Dr. Canhu said it was urgent that we leave in the morning to begin our work.

Later that afternoon, *Meelj'ak Chamel*, the local witchcraft doctor, approached us. She said we should not leave without protecting ourselves from illness, and she wanted to perform a cleansing ceremony for us. The locals respected witchcraft and would usually see the *ak'bil* (witch) before seeing a doctor. We agreed to the cleansing ceremony mainly for the local people to see us following their custom, knowing that would give them more trust in our ideas. That evening, we came together and took part in the washing observance in a large three-sided lean-to, just outside of town. I could *ik'* (smell) something like incense burning. We were asked to *piko* (prick) our finger and leave one drop of blood in a vessel on the altar. I looked at Marcos and Abre, and they nodded to go ahead. I followed in line, pricked my finger and left a drop of blood. After the finger pricking, we formed a half circle and watched Meelj'ak perform a brief ceremony. She asked us to repeat a chant she spoke. After repeating the chant several times, a man brought in a live chicken. Meelj'ak took the chicken, said a few words, then cut off its head, letting it bleed into the vessel that held our drops of blood. After a few more minutes of chanting, the ceremony was over, and we walked back to town.

I asked Ma'k about the ceremony. What had just happened? He explained the importance of *ch'olan* (sacrifice) in the Mayan culture and said they sacrificed the chicken to a spirit in exchange for our health and safe passage.

I shared an atut with Marcos for the night and in the morning; we left on a *tajbe* (path) to one of the small villages a short distance away. When we arrived, tables were set up to hand out medicine and leaflets about cleanliness. The leaflets, showed how to keep areas of the home clean and in pictograms the importance of keeping animals out of the eating and cooking areas. Abre and Dr. Canhu went to outlying houses to care for the sick who could not travel to us in Bachajon.

My job was to show the *ck'inil* (children) how to wash their hands. I taught them to count from one to ten twice while they washed their hands, this was the time recommended for cleanliness. *Jun (1), che'b (2), oxe'b (3), chane'b (4), job'b (5), waque'b (6), juque'b (7), waxaqu'b (8), balune'b (9)* and *lajune'b (10)*. Being a tall, redheaded, white guy making funny faces while counting to ten kept their attention. When we were done, I pulled out my frisbee, a new toy for them, and we played for hours.

Dr. Canhu returned alone, leaving Abre to spend the night with patients who were sick enough to be on IV liquids. That night, Padre "A" was preparing to say

Mass for the people who had passed. The women were preparing the Boa Constrictor we had brought as a gift for dinner. The snake was prepared in several ways. One was a stew type dish, snake meat mixed with cornmeal and chilies that were eaten with small fat empanadas. The other was meat cut into long strips and roasted until the meat was crispy. After dark, each one in our group was a guest in a different home throughout the town. In the morning, they served eggs with tomatoes, sweet fruits from the forest and *kahpe* (coffee).

We gathered at a church in the center of the village for Padre "A" to say Mass. Giving a sermon in the forest was a language challenge. Padre "A" had to speak using over four dialects, finding words that overlapped one another. After mass Abre went to check on the people that were on IVs, Dr. Canhu selected several people in the village to teach them how and when to administer medications. Dr. Canhu was determined to reach another village before dark; we loaded up and took off. As we traveled further south we were deeper in the lowlands of the rainforest. The lowland forest is rainier and more jungle like. We passed over several small creeks and walked parallel to a crystal-clear lake. I worried Muk'ul dak would find more *ajch'al* (mud) but luckily, there was no deep mud. Our destination was close to the lake, I looked forward to being able to swim, bathe, and to see my reflection in the water. I had not seen a mirror in a week. There also was a possibility of having a meal of fresh fish.

We arrived in the next small village early the next afternoon, early enough for Dr. Canhu and Abre to set up our traveling clinic. Ma'k, my guide helped me translate directions to a lake close by. He did not trust me to find the lake by myself, so both Ma'k and Marcos decided to join me for a *nux* (swim). We reached the lake, with two small waterfalls flowing into a *lush*(lagoon). The waterfall was the perfect height to stand under and shower.

Marcos said fish is a staple in the Chw diet and we will eat fish for dinner. Ma'k was off arranging for our clothes to be laundered. We hit the jackpot in this village. Ma'k found me find me a pair of white baggy pants to wear while my clothes were being cleaned. I was a foot and a half taller than most men in the region. The pant leg came up far above my calves, practically to my knees. When Dr. Canhu and Abre returned, I told Abre about showering at the falls. She had not bathed in days. Ma'K quickly found several women to escort Abre to the lake. When Abre heard about the laundry deal Ma'K arranged, she was thrilled.

We were served a unique and tasty fish dinner. Fresh-water fish from the local lake, with a fruit chutney made from inga, zapotes, sapotes, mango and other local fruits. The chutney was spiced with just the right amount of dried chili. The next morning, we went through the same exercise as the day before, treating people for diarrhea and *k'ajk* (fever). We spent most of the morning at the clinic, then packed up our gear and headed toward Chilon, a municipality further southwest of Bachajon.

Mak'ul dak was getting restless and wanted to leave. Somehow *Mak'ul dak's* agitation made me feel edgy and sad. There were times I just did not know what I was doing here, in the southern Mexican jungle, with people so different from me, and all the difficulties of navigating life and language. I enjoyed the absence of chaos at home in California. I left behind all the negative things I had experienced at home. The failures in school, behavior problems, and seizures that left me and my father far apart and unable to connect. The separation from my siblings was painful, not only the physical distance but the emotional distance created, with me being the weird brother with some sort of bizarre epilepsy that few people understood. Being here, with these people was so far away from all of that. But the sadness and loneliness never really left me. More times than I liked to admit, thoughts and feelings of loss and failure filled me with a deep sorrow. I wondered if people still talked about me? Was I still loved? Forgotten by my friends? Did I have a real future? Could I ever return to California? I wouldn't allow myself to sink into sadness and become depressed when these questions came up. I could only stand-up, shake it off and move on.

Continuing on the path to Chilon another twenty miles from Bachajon, we traveled on a dirt path until we reached Chilon, there the path turned into a wider dirt and mud road that was used by old beat-up trucks to pick up coffee, sometimes produce, jungle fruits and crafts made in the mountains and villages in the Highlands. When starting down a steep mountain, we could see coffee trees, full of fruit and almost ready to pick. Marcos and Ma'k reminded me that when we returned to Sitala, we would celebrate coffee season, reminding me I would also be picking coffee. As we continued, Marcos pulled up on his mule and rode closer to me. He began speaking to me in his teacher's voice about our location.

We were on the border of the *Selva Lacandon*, Lacandon Jungle, a jungle that spreads out across two million acres, and is home to countless wildlife, plants, fish, and insects. The Lacandon Jungle is only populated by 700 to 900 people. The Lacandon people are a very secluded and private tribe and remain one of the most primitive societies living on Earth. We were now in their territory. We will be coming up to the Ugsumacinta river that borders Chiapas and the Lacondon Jungle. Marcos assured me that as long as we stayed on the North side of the river, we were not within their territory and would be safe. Continuing on a path along the river I was surrounded by lagoons, waterfalls, and lush rainforest. The sound of birds, howler monkeys and other animals was deafening.

We continued until we came across what appeared to be a Lacandon family of five walking on the trail. Marcos and Dr. Canhu both looked surprised. They said it's uncommon for a Lacandon woman and her children to leave their homes in the heart of the jungle. The Lacandon family was dressed in their native clothing, a seamless, white, full-length garment. They looked frightened as we approached. They spoke Hacht'an or Jachta'an, a Lacandon dialect. Marcos looked at Dr. Canhu, Abre, and Ma'K to see if anyone spoke their dialect. They all shook their heads no. Marcos said he knew a little and would give it a try. Marcos greeted them saying *ba'ax ka wa'alik* (hello how are you) in hacht'an. It worked, they responded.

Marcos tried his best to communicate, although he was not fluent in their language. Dr. Canhu told me there were fewer than twenty-five people in the world outside the jungle who spoke *Hacht'an*. After a few minutes, Marcos decoded that the child's mother was saying that one of her children was ill and experiencing k'uxjolol (headache) and k'ajk (fever). Dr. Canhu did not see the sick child with the group. They had left the child at the home of others. We all agreed we would go to the child.

This experience of going out of our way to help others on the trail happened over and over. It was such a simple act of kindness, and it felt unconscious and instinctive to go out of our way to aid others. The compassion the people we met showed one another still brings a tear to my eye. More than fifty years later, as I write this, I am still learning about kindheartedness and how kindness brings us together.

We arrived at a shelter with only three sides, the walls covered with various grasses, and supported by roughhewn wood poles. Eight to ten people stood in front of their home, shy and reserved. They knew we were there for no other reason than to help the sick child. After the welcoming, they began preparing a meal and organizing shelter for all of us. Dr. Canhu and Abre attended to the sick child who had an internal infection which was treated.

That evening, Dr Canhu sat next to me. In his empathetic manner, he complimented me for helping Abre and how I was handling myself on this trip, as an eighteen-year-old American kid, so out of place in the highlands. He said that he'd seen me experience several seizures while we were traveling. I asked how I behaved during a seizure. His description of the seizure was no different from others'. Dr. Canhu chuckled and said he was not a neurologist or brain surgeon, but he would do his best to understand. I'm not fluent in Spanish medical vocabulary but I explained what I knew about the history of my seizures. I told Dr Canhu about the diagnosis of front temporal lobe epilepsy. He had little knowledge of epilepsy besides grand mal and petit mal seizures, but he was aware of brain research happening at a rapid pace throughout the world.

He described to me how epilepsy is dealt with in the Mayan culture. As Abre had explained to me, the Mayans believe that epilepsy is the struggle between the animal and the human spirit within us. This is usually the spirit of the jaguar or the armadillo seeking revenge for being hunted.

The Tzeltal Indians call epilepsy *tubik'al* and treat it with two forest roots, *tsim'o* and *wewr'u*. A shaman must administer these herbs in a religious ceremony which includes animal sacrifice. The Mayans view epilepsy as incurable but believe it can be controlled through the combination of a shaman and herbal medicine.

The *ochloko'haxoh* (fits or seizures) I have differed from grand mal or a convulsive type of seizure. Dr. Canhu did not know if the Tzeltal had a name for my type of seizure. He suspected it would derive from a less aggressive spirit and a different animal spirit. Dr. Canhu recognized the need for medication dealing with epilepsy in the rainforest. Anti-seizure medication is available to treat epilepsy, but the side effects had been difficult for many, people preferred the ancient ways of dealing with the disease. He asked if I was interested in talking to a Tzeltal shaman. When I hesitated, he laughed and said stay on the medicine you're on. He assured me he would look after me when we were together.

We stayed in the small lean-to for several more days while the boy was healing, then we loaded up to head back to Yajalon, about ten miles away. Passing through the jungle, we saw howling monkeys calling out to one another, making so much noise you could barely hear the sounds of birds or the wind blowing through the trees. We exited the jungle to the more familiar landscape of the highlands and coffee trees in full bloom. Coffee trees have a small white flower with a sweet scent. The fragrance of the flowers is overwhelming when the wind blows in the right direction.

We arrived at our destination after lunch. Yajalon was bustling with activity. Families, farmers, livestock owners, everyone coming to the center of town to sell, to buy and trade. There are many handcrafts, farm tools, pots, pans, and other essentials. Yajalon has access to a road leading to Tuxtla and beyond, making it the commercial hub for the jungle and nearby municipalities. When we picked coffee in Sitala, the coffee came to Yajalon for distribution. Trucks came to town once a week.

We seemed to have arrived on a special day, maybe a Saint's Day or a local holiday. People were out enjoying themselves. Father A and I headed to the other side of the park where I saw a man wearing a large papier mache bull costume, completely covered with firecrackers. Music started playing, and a fuse was lit as people gathered to watch. The poor little guy in the costume began dancing around like a bull while hundreds of firecrackers went off within inches of him. The surrounding crowd was yelling and applauding and dancing alongside him. I had been to many festivals but had never seen this firecracker dance. Dr Canhu and Abre were both familiar with this dance and had probably attended to people hurt while dancing.

Dr. Canhu and Abre headed over to the clinic where the director offered us whatever we needed to resupply our own surgery back in Sitala. Father A went to the rectory and church. I helped unpack the horses and mules. Then I followed *j'a'tels* (workers) back to the festival. Nobody spoke Spanish and I was not able to keep up with the dialects being spoken. I left the other men and followed Marcos and Ma'k to a fruit stand. Ma'k picked up one variety and handed the fruit to me. I stared at it for a moment and heard people say *ik' ik'* (smell it, smell it). Ma'k took out his knife, cut open the orange pear shaped fruit and held it up to my nose. The fruit smelled terrible, like a rotten potato. Then all I heard was *k'us k'us* (eat, eat); people gathered to watch me take a bite. I thought it must be a trick. Ma'k took a bite and so did I. It smelled bad but tasted sweet, like a banana and cantaloupe in one with a blood red color. Everyone was waiting for my response. I looked up and shouted *iek iek* (good, good).

Chapter 16

Coffee Harvest

In a few days, we'd be back in Sitala. I was ready to get there. My butt was sore from being on the back of Muk'ul dak for three months. When we arrived back at Sitala, the unloading began, distributing the medication and straightening up the clinic. The women were dressed in fresh new k'uil (skirts) with traditional hand embroidery with Tzeltal and Mayan symbols. Being back was cause for celebration and a special meal was being prepared by the women. Turkey, squash, monkey stew and fresh forest fruit were being served. The air was fresh, moist, and a spirit of friendliness filled the air. I thought how exciting it would be to have my family there, to experience where I am living and how well I am doing.

The kajpej (coffee) harvest had started. Ma'K asked if I wanted to join him in the uxoj (coffee picking) in the morning? I responded with excitement, yes. Ma'k said we had to gather supplies. We needed a *chim pah*, a dual saddle bag that fits over a donkey or mule and *koxtal*, a bag that fits over one's shoulder to carry the coffee from the trees back to the pack animal. I collected my ch'op and u'kop (water jug and eating bowl) and was ready to go along with twenty or thirty men, women and children starting off on a path to the hillsides. Coffee trees in the highlands do not grow on a ranch or plantation; they grow scattered on the hillsides and in the canyons. There were many trees and sometimes it was tricky to reach them. The *te'el kajpej* (coffee tree) is not a big tree. It is short and mixed in with thick vegetation. The ground was slippery with mud. I brought Muk'ul dak as he was more surefooted than I was. We reached our destination not far from the *ch'iwich* (center of town). The men and women and *ch'inil* (teenagers) were ready with their bags and headed up the side of a hill. I stayed Muk'ul dak, sitting up high to get a good look at how this was done. Ma'k encouraged me to join them. I assured him I would be there shortly. It was good to observe the situation and learn any techniques I could pick up before starting. I had humiliated myself too many times by jumping right in without having a good look at what was going on.

I jumped off my mule, put on my bags, and headed up the side of the hill. Ten seconds later, I slipped in the mud and fell down.

Ma'k shouted out, "Take off your shoes."

I should have noticed that no one else had shoes on. I took my tennis shoes off and started back up the hillside, still slipping and sliding. Everyone started shouting *ch'opemih, ch'opemih*, but I did not know what they were saying, until Ma'k yelled, "Dig your toes in the mud."

That was a great suggestion, and I started to climb more easily. I must have looked like such an amateur coffee picker. I thought I was doing it right, picking a few beans and putting them into the bag. A picker close to me said to me *pik pik* (Feel the beans with both your fingers and hands). Ma'k came over with an expert to show me. To start, you position your koxtal at the end of your elbow. You wiggle your fingers quickly through the leaves and leaf stems. The beans fall off in a steady roll down your forearm, hit the curve of the inside of the elbow and if bent just right, they fall into the koxtal. I spent most of the day trying to perfect this technique.

We ate lunch and *uk'ih* (drinks in a social grouping). We drank a fruit juice the women prepared for us. Tzeltal Indians drink very little alcohol outside of celebrations. Of course, all the chit-chatting during our meal was about how awkward I was picking coffee. This type of soft talk about me was thousands of times less stressful and less hurtful than being teased in a school lunchroom. The last few years living in Mexico had taught me one very important thing: you cannot feel bad laughing at yourself. Making it fun to learn a new culture and language is the only way to go.

The *uxoj* (coffee harvest) continued for another several weeks. I did not go out to pick every day. I often thought I was in the way, not physically, but I was in the way of the *j'a'tel* (workers) concentrating on picking., they loved watching me fumble with the coffee beans. The second phase of the harvest was ready, collecting the picked coffee and putting it into koxtal's (burlap gunny sacks) and storing the coffee in an *otel* (covered food storage stall). The coffee would stay in storage until it was moved to Bachajon, where a truck would pick it up to take to a distribution center.

With the coffee in storage, I returned to work with Abre in the clinic. Abre said, I heard you enjoyed your experience of picking coffee. I agreed it was a fascinating experience. She said that she thought the experience of the people working alongside you was more fascinating than the time that I had. I laughed and agreed. Another shipment of pharmaceutical samples had been airdropped, and I was busy sorting out sample medicine.

It was only a week or so until we had to move the coffee, as Marcos had received notice the truck was making its way to Bachajon. We loaded up the mules, donkeys, and horses with koxtals full of coffee weighing at least one hundred pounds each. We ran out of room and had to *kuch ta patel* (carry on one's back). We didn't have to walk all the way to Bachajon. There was a path that led to a place in the road where we knew the truck would be passing by. We left very early one morning, horses, mules, donkeys, and men working as hard as the mules. We got to our destination and gathered *taj* (pine needles) to sleep on. We planned to spend the night so we wouldn't miss the truck coming by. We ate *uc'ohmac'il* (cornmeal water and sugar) and fruit for dinner. In the morning, we waited for the truck on the side of the dirt road. We had no idea when the truck was coming. We stood a few yards off the path and moved closer to the road so we would be noticed. We stood up for an hour or so when I decided to *emt'ejam* (sit down), I immediately heard *tea'el* (stand) because of all the insects and spiders on the ground. After standing for another hour, I was shifting my weight from foot-to-foot shuffling around. People were looking at me saying I'm *ajk'ot* (dancing). Marcos and Ma'k came over and said I was not standing correctly. Ma'k brought over one of the men to demonstrate how to stand. Ma'k told me to stand with my legs spread evenly with my shoulders, to push my knees back and push my thighs forward slightly and put a smile on my face. I locked my legs like a horse does when it is sleeping. I could not believe how comfortable I was. I stood in the same position for another hour.

Ma'k said to me, "Now you have time to listen to the birds, monkeys and the noise of the wind blowing through the trees."

This is one lesson I still use today whenever standing in a line. People look at me funny whenever I take this stance, and I see them moving their bodies all over and always think of the word ajk'ot. After eating our cornmeal lunch, all the men, women, and children stood in a single line. There was a straight dead tree across the road. The tree cast a long narrow shadow, everyone stood in the tree's shadow to get shade from the hot sun. As the sun moved through the sky, the shadow moved, and so did we. We must have looked like a human sundial. After several hours, the truck arrived., men started shouting *t'olaj* (pile it on). We unloaded the bags from the animals and loaded them onto the truck. There was an argument during the money exchange for the coffee, but it was resolved peaceably, and the truck went on its way to pick up more coffee. The uxoj was complete for the year. We returned to Sitala the next day where there was a *k'in* (fiesta), party for all the participants of the coffee harvest. Food, drink, music, and dancing.

Chapter 17

Padre "A" and Birth Certificates

Padre "A" invited me to visit the church in Sitala. I had been in the church many times but never had a personal tour. The church was built in the early 1940s by the local community and added onto several times. There were carvings throughout, statues representing the twelve Stations of the Cross, the Virgin Mary, and many saints. There was a large baptismal, carved from a single piece of wood, a ten-foot wooden cross over the altar and a pair of hand built and carved entrance doors, handmade by local *tsi'wil* (wood workers). I had met some of these men but with no idea of the skills they possessed to produce this magnificent work. The church had a dirt floor, swept daily, mopped occasionally, and patched with a mud compound when needed which made the floor as smooth as concrete. The exterior was mud plaster and whitewashed. The three bells in the bell tower, which probably weighed four hundred pounds each, were donated by a church in San Cristobal and carried over fifty miles through the rainforest to Sitala. It took over a month to bring the bells back to Sitala. The bells are rung three times per day to announce Mass, in the morning, at noon, and in the evening.

After the tour, we talked again about my life in California and in Jalapa before coming to Chiapas. We had traveled together for months, and he was fully aware of me staring into space with a *luylum sitill* (twitch on my face and eyelid). He understood how my seizures were stigmatized and acknowledged how hurtful that must have been. He did not understand why I left my family but understood how life in general must have been difficult, being shamed and humiliated for having a disease no one could explain. I could only tell him that when I had an opportunity to escape and look for something, anything, to change the way I was living I took it. Padre "A" knew I had found peace in this accepting Tzeltal community, as a guest in the rainforest. Priests, doctors, nurses, and all outsiders are guests. If you're not a Tzeltal Indian, your visit is only temporary. He was not asking me to leave, only reminding me this was not my home and someday I must leave.

Our conversation moved to the work he was doing in Chiapas. Padre "A" began with the history of discrimination, slavery, lack of medical care and government supported schools. Our history is not very different from how the American Indians were treated in your country. The Mexican government promised the Mayan and Aztec people hospitals, schools, roads, agriculture equipment, and running water. Promises were seldom kept. One of our biggest problems is obtaining birth certificates for our children. Without birth certificates, the census does not reflect the real population and municipalities lose medical care and funding for schools. People without a birth certificate are not even allowed to leave the State of Chiapas. To receive a birth certificate, people must go to a state records office and speak in Spanish, not their native Tzeltal language. The nearest record office can be days away and have fees they don't have. Padre "A" said he is working with Abre and Marcos to legislate for the ability to issue birth certificates here at the clinic.

It is the position of a Jesuit priest to not only be the church's priest but the protector of the people's human rights. In Bachajon, Chilon and Yajalon small craft industries are developing so men and women making crafts could earn money. So often they were treated poorly, cheated out of money and had the supplies they were promised stolen. I was surprised when he told me he knew and worked with my Uncle Bill, Padre Nolan. Padre "A" worked closely with my uncle, in the area of human rights. My uncle was a large and muscular man and had no problem using his size to intimidate those trying to steal from or take advantage of the Tzeltal. After our long discussion, he concluded, "Your uncle was a very respected and much-loved priest. He may have been a better protector of the people than a missionary priest. That may have been why he was transferred to Brazil. You should be very proud of him."

Life went on in the rainforest. I was working at the clinic, bathing and swimming in the rivers and lagoons. I took walks in the forest and learned about the plants, trees, and fruits. I continued trying to perfect my use of the slingshot but there was no way I was going to be able to shoot the stem off the mango fruit at fifteen feet and then catch the fruit before it hit the ground anytime soon. I was the best frisbee player and could throw it longer than anyone. The younger boys and girls liked helping me with the language. They always laughed when I pronounced a word wrong or could not get a particular sound correct.

Life was good, but still I wondered about home and how everyone was doing and how my life would eventually work out. I had had no contact with my family for well over a year and I was sure my mother would be worried about me and how I was managing my seizures. I wished I could comfort her, letting her know how well I was doing, and the happiness and peace I had found here.

One month in the clinic, we must have delivered more than ten babies, all healthy. Abre wanted the babies to have birth certificates as soon as possible and she discussed with Padre "A" her idea of him taking the birth certificates to the state records offices in San Cristobal to be certified. Padre "A" asked me to go with him on this six-day round trip, and we agreed to leave the following week. We needed Muk'ul dak, another mule for Padre "A," one pack donkey and three helpers. We had everything packed and ready by the end of the week. Our trip to San Cristobal was uneventful. Padre knew many people; we always had a place to stay along the way. Padre "A" said Mass wherever we stopped, and when we arrived in San Cristobal, we stayed at the church rectory.

The discrimination was evident immediately as we entered the state records office. The officials were not at all interested in why we were there and questioned us as to why the parents of the children were not there themselves. They also questioned Abre's credentials. Padre "A" went back to the rectory and brought over one of the local priests. The local priest knew one of the officials and was able to facilitate the process so that we could get the birth certificates. Padre "A" knew I was interested in the anthropology of the Mayan Indians and said we could take an alternate route home to see one of the smaller Mayan ruins that had never been uncovered.

Padre "A" said mass at the cathedral before we left for home. We reached the ruins on the second day. This site was only comprised of two stone structures. Our three helpers unpacked their machetes and began cutting back vegetation for us to get closer. Padre "A" was as interested as I was in exploring the site, we both were pulling back brush to see the art and inscriptions on the faces of the stone buildings. We didn't know exactly what we were looking at and could only guess at the probable uses of buildings. After we were there for an hour or so, one of the j'a'tel (workers) came up to us with a ring he had found. The ring was made of bone with a flat top and a symbol carved into it. This was a real treasure, a real finding. Padre "A" looked closely and suggested that it was a ceremonial ring and the hieroglyphics on the ring could mean water, "ja" in Mayan. The same symbols were found on the stone faces of many of the ancient buildings. Ancient Mayan language was written using symbols, not words. Padre "A" handed me the ring and said it is yours. I still have it today.

We ate lunch leaning against a tree just trying to see and feel what life must have been like here 2000 years ago. Although we were anxious to get back and deliver the hard-won birth certificates, we traveled slowly through the mountains and gorges, passing people on the trail, stopping to see how they were and if they needed our help. Twice that day Padre "A" said mass for people on the trail, the groups of people numbering only four or five. The landscape was full of switchbacks, and we could see people across the canyons we encountered. Later that day we spotted a man on a horse on the other side of a gulch. He was on a large palomino horse, his silver spurs and decorative chaps sparkling in the sun. I could see that the men with us were getting nervous and began talking more to one another.

Padre "A" pulled up close to me and said the men were frightened. The man we spotted had stolen, physically abused and cheated many people and owed many of them for coffee, fruit, and clothing. He had charged exorbitant prices for thread used in making clothing and the intricate hand embroidered pieces they had made. He was also known for stealing medicine and medical supplies from various clinics in the region. Padre "A" also recognized him as someone who had fought for more government control of the Tzeltal people. He did not want the government spending money on education and the vaccine project in the highlands of Chiapas. His name was Senor Alfonso. We continued until we met up with him. After Padre "A" and Senor Alfonso chatted for a few minutes Padre "A" hinted to me and the others to back up a bit and move off the path. Padre "A" asked Alfonso to look at something on the other side of the canyon, and when Alfonso turned his head to look over, Padre "A" pulled out a large pistol from his saddlebag and shot Alfonso. His pistol was so big it actually blew his head off to one side. The gun shot rang through the canyons of the forest, birds shrieked and the *chapin's* (monkeys) screamed. One of the men ran over to Alfonso, stared at his lifeless body saying *anima, anima* (dead, dead). A man had just been killed in cold blood eight feet from me, leaving blood splatter on my shirt, and me in disbelief and shock over what I had just witnessed. The men stood there, quietly, fully aware that a *fmilaw* (murder) had taken place.

There was also a sense of *k'in* (festival) in the air, a sense that something *iek* (good) may have happened. Without talking or planning, Alfonso's dead body was *kil* (dragged) to the side of the deep canyon and dropped off. The men were talking among themselves and though I didn't understand all that was being said, the gist of it was that Senior Alfonso was at fault, not Padre "A."

Alfonso's body would decompose quickly, and his belongings would probably never be found. His horse now belonged to whoever wanted him. Quietly, we continued the *tajbe* (path) to home. I never heard anyone mention the *chaim* (death) of Senior Alfonso again, and I have never revealed the real name of Padre "A."

After thinking about it for a long time, I was eventually okay with what I witnessed that day in the canyon. It may not have been right, but if it satisfied a wrong, maybe it was acceptable. Padre "A" reminded me his job was to protect the people who did not have the means to protect themselves. I always felt uneasy with what I witnessed, but I came to accept his action as the law of the jungle.

We made it back to Sitala before dark, and were welcomed back with food, drink, and music. Our trip was over. The birth certificates were delivered to Abre.

Chapter 18

Planning to Exit the Highlands

I wanted to talk to Abre about everything I'd been thinking about since the trip to San Cristobal and my conversations with Padre "A" about my future. She was so busy at the clinic it was difficult finding time, but when the opportunity arose, we talked for a long time about my past and family. Abre convinced me she knew and had seen how strong and healthy I was even though I had seizures. She understood that my parents did not comprehend what I had experienced through much of my life. Abre thought my behavior problems at home were because of my constant failures while growing up and my sense that my parents expected me to set an example to the other kids since I was the oldest. My brothers and sister were successful in school, had friends, and had healthy relationships with our parents. She believed my leaving home, being alone when Uncle Bill left, finding myself in the isolation of Sitala was like a shock treatment for me. I had only myself to rely on throughout my travels in Mexico and my life in Sitala, and I found out how capable I was of finding success at every turn, not failure. Through all my experiences I was able to discover who I was: a competent and intelligent young man. This has been a steep mountain to climb.

She suggested I go back to California for a while, see my family and friends, and learn what opportunities might be there for me and I could see my doctor and find out if anything had changed in treatment protocols. I am always welcome back to Sitala, she said, and my heart cracked open with the love I felt.

I wasn't sure what was going on at home. For all I knew, my family had moved. I would not know until I got to a location with a telephone. I met with Marcos and Ma'k to tell them it was time for me to leave. They both praised me on how I could interact with everyone, how well I was doing with learning their language, and how much the help I provided working in the clinic had benefited the community. I had promised to help complete the building of the new *otel* (food stall) one that would keep the animals out. I was looking forward to working with the *tsi'wil's* (woodworkers) on this project, building wooden structures using machetes, axes, and other primitive means of building. Even though I was ready to leave, it would be a month before another airplane landed in Sitala.

Starting to feel excited to return home, I knew I now had the confidence to meet the challenges of reintroducing myself to my family. There were no more problems in controlling my behavior and I was no longer afraid of being out of control. Through becoming more aware of when I seized, I knew when there had been a gap or lapse of time and was able to put these intervals and the tiredness, I felt afterwards together to suspect I'd had a seizure. I was no longer struggling to find out who I was. After what I had experienced, leaving home at fifteen, and making it three thousand miles to the most southern state of Mexico, I knew that wherever I was in this world, I would be ok, I could survive and succeed anywhere.

Over the next month, I had many people to say farewell to. That month I heard Abre call out so many times *tojkes* (help). I was running between the otel and the clinic all day. As weeks went by, I felt sad. I was leaving the people and the place that had changed my life in so many significant ways. The people of Sitala had accepted me as the person I was, not a person with an illness or a disability. I still carry with me all the lessons I learned from them; how to stand without dancing, keep a smile while working, learn by example, and most importantly to be kind.

How could I say goodbye when there is no word for goodbye? The Mayan, Tzeltal people have no word for hello or goodbye. There is no hello because you do not really leave. You greet people by saying *bin awilel* (how are you) instead of how you have been. In our transient culture, this is a strange concept; to think that someone has always been there, you are just checking in to see how they are doing. The same with goodbye, when leaving you say *bolconish* (I'm stepping out), and they respond *de sa wileb* (good traveling). There is no goodbye when you never left.

I wanted to bring back a few items, of course, my *uh'ap* (eating bowl), my *pixjola* (hat) and *qejch'* (a strap that goes over your forehead to help to carry things on your back) and the Mayan ring. I would have liked to bring many things but only had so much room.

I did grab a handful of coffee beans I had picked and threw them in my backpack.

I was so nervous in those last few weeks. Will I be welcomed? What would they expect from me and how would my father react to me? After all, I was still having seizures. How would I get home? My visa had expired months ago, and I would have to cross the border without documents. I was bringing back a few artifacts that were restricted. I couldn't fly on a commercial plane back to the states without an ID. I decide to hitchhike and take the bus. Once I am out of the highlands, it will take me another week to get to the border.

My last week in Sitala, I played with the *alnich'an* (children), shared meals with many families and friends, many of whom I had cared for in the clinic. I gave my frisbee to the children and I left my Swiss army knife with Marcos. Abre got my personal Swiss army first aid kit. The elders had me over one last time, I did not make the mistake I had on my arrival of swallowing the water but when I was offered more of their jungle moonshine I refused.

The single engine Cessna was expected at the end of the week. I assumed the pilot had received the message and was ready for me to fly back with him. The pilot would bring medical supplies and I spent time with Abre organizing shelves for the refreshed supplies coming in.

Just like when I had landed before, the entire community came out to the landing field and cleared and picked up anything that might interfere with the plane landing. I heard the plane coming in over the mountain making one pass with the pilots arm out the window waving, circling back and landing. I helped unload the plane and once again said I'm leaving for a while, not goodbye. The children were pulling at my pant legs, telling me not to go. The older men and women sat off to the side and gave me a gentle wave.

As we boarded the plane the pilot told me we would stop in Chilon for the night as he had medical supplies for the clinic there. That sounded good to me as it was getting late in the afternoon. It would be smart to not try and fly over the mountains in the dark. We landed in Chilon an hour later. The pilot must have known the people there very well as we were greeted with first class hospitality. Chilon Is larger than Sitala, with many more buildings in the center of town. When I traveled through Chilon with Marcos, Dr. Chun, Padre "A," Abre and six men on horses and mules, we must have looked dirty, hungry, and worn. At that time, we were welcomed, nicely fed, and given shelter. This visit was several marks above the last visit with better food, and entertainment of music and dancing performed by the children. The pilot, Tomas, and I were clean and brought gifts, denim pants for the teenagers, and toys for the children.

Before we left in the morning, Tomas wanted to take a swim in a nearby lagoon. I joined him, soaking in the warmth and beauty for the last time. Tomas and I checked out the plane and got ready to take off. The field was clear, the weather was cloudy, but okay for flying. We took off, heading north at a low altitude so we could keep an eye out for the navigational landmarks.

After several hours, we made our approach into Tuxtla Gutierrez, the capital of Chiapas. It was starting to rain, so I went into the terminal to find a pay phone. Nervously, I made an international phone call home to talk to my parents. International calls at that time were expensive and I called collect to save the small amount of money I had left. My brother Mark, now seventeen, answered the phone, and I told him I was coming home. I asked how things were going and if everyone was alright. He said all was well. Gary got a concussion on the football field but was recovering. I was happy to get a little background before speaking to my mother. Mom picked up the phone and immediately wanted to know how I was and when I was coming home. It was two years since I had heard her voice and was comforted by it. I could hear my father in the background grumbling about the cost of the international phone call, and of course how I was. Mom said to hurry home. She had good news about a doctor she had met. I told them I would be home in a week and would call when I reached the border. In true Gernandt fashion, she ended with "We will have a party."

I decided to hitchhike to the Pacific Coast from Tuxtla, and I got a ride on a large semi-truck, much nicer and safer than the crazy ride I had taken on the oil tanker on my way to Sitala. The driver, who was a veritable chatterbox, had a habit of always looking at me while talking, and not paying attention to the highway. I kept hinting to him to notice the oncoming traffic, but with no success. Somehow, we arrived safely at the Pacific coast, and I planned to continue north on the coastal route to the border.

I had not sat down to a meal other than the Tzeltal diet of corn, squash, jungle fruit, turkey, pork and bushmeat for several years. I chose a small restaurant along the bay sitting at a full height table and chair, placing my order for a more typical Mexican meal of enchiladas, rice, and beans.

After lunch, taking a break on the boardwalk, and watching the ocean, I worried about my mother mentioning a doctor in our phone call. Starting the cycle of seeing doctors, new medicines and constantly being monitored was not my intention in coming home. That my father did not even get on the phone, made me think he was hesitant for me to return. I was not the same ill, out of control, son who was returning, and I needed to convince my father that I was fine, even though I had epilepsy. I wanted and really needed him to be proud of me for all I had accomplished.

I let these negative thoughts float away, stood up, remembered to put on a smile and enjoy the moment. I pulled out my map and planned my route back to the Mexican border town of Tijuana. It was a long trip, over three thousand miles.

A taxi drove me back to the highway where it would be easy to hitch a ride. Hitchhiking was a lot safer in those days, most people were friendly, and they always wanted my story. I learned a few tricks for long distance hitchhiking: if it's late in the day, I would make sure they were traveling far enough so I would not be dropped off at night in the middle of nowhere. One of my best trips was outside of Tehuantepec. A Mexican family of four in an old station wagon picked me up as it was getting dark, and they insisted that I come to their home with them. They fed me, gave me a bedroom to sleep in and in the morning, drove me back to the highway. The memories I hold of hitchhiking in Mexico, with few exceptions, are of meeting the kindest and most generous people. I was a teenager and people may have picked me up because they were worried about my well-being. Traveling was slow, roads along the coast were variable, but I stayed on schedule, and over the next week, I worked my way to the border.

Part Four

Chapter 19

Back in the USA

After five years of traveling throughout Mexico and living in the highlands of Chiapas, a journey I will never forget or regret, I arrived in Mexicali, a border town a few hours from Tijuana. I called home, told my father that I had lost my visa and needed help to get smuggled across the US border. He told me he had been eagerly waiting for my call for over a week and I expressed how excited I was to see him and the family. My father enjoyed adventure and was excited to help me cross the border without my visa. We agreed to meet me at the Tijuana central bus station the next day at two o'clock in the afternoon. I spent the night at an inexpensive hotel and in the morning, I bought a ticket for the two-hour bus ride to Tijuana.

I stood outside the entrance of the bus station waiting for my dad. My father's car would be easy to spot; he always drove a big new Oldsmobile, four-door sedan, the classic American salesman's car. My father was compulsive about being on time. At two o'clock, I saw his car, grabbed my backpack off the sidewalk and jumped in the front seat, giving my dad a huge hug and smile. He returned the same. At that moment, I knew he was going to give me a chance to prove myself. Maybe we could have a real new beginning. Before I could say another word, he excitedly said, "I have a plan."

We stopped for lunch at a small taqueria, my last meal in Mexico for some time. We went to a Mexican tourist store on the way out of town, bought a Mexican sombrero and headed for the border crossing. In the seventies you did not need a visa or passport if you were only in Mexico for the day. When we drove up to the border crossing, the officer leaned over and asked, "What are you bringing with you and how long have you been in Mexico?"

Totally relaxed, my father said a few gifts to my kids. We have only been here for the day. With a pleasant smile, the guard waved us through, and we drove across the border into the United States. The plan worked perfectly: my father had smuggled me across the border. Two more hours till I arrive home.

I was getting excited to see my brothers and my sister and, of course, my mom. Dad and I had a pleasant conversation during the drive, though it became clear there was no way I could tell him in two hours what I had done over the last two and a half years since we had seen each other. I told him we would have to do this in stages. As we continued talking, I started forgetting English words. I was afraid that after speaking Spanish and Tzeltal for so long I had forgotten my native language. My father laughed at my forgetfulness. He assured me my bedroom was waiting for me and the house had changed little, I began to think my fears about our relationship were maybe exaggerated; so far, we were getting along. I was glad to hear how well my brothers were doing in school and sports. My sister Annie, now a teenager, was enjoying all her friends and a new boyfriend. Mom was concerned about her brother. Uncle Bill was in Brazil at that time and doubting his faith in the Catholic Church and thinking of leaving. Bill leaving the church was upsetting for mom as she had built her identity in the community around him being a priest. Being the head of the missionary group supporting Bill, would be over and the prestige of having a brother who is a Jesuit priest, would be gone. I was also interested in his well-being; if not for him, I would never have gone to Mexico. In so many ways, he'd fulfilled the role of father for me.

When we reached the freeway off ramp to La Habra, my hometown my anxiety ramped up in anticipation of arriving home and seeing everyone. The closer we came to the house, the more I worried I would forget English words and be teased and laughed at. We pulled into the driveway, and before we even came to a complete stop, Mom ran out to deliver me her long-awaited hug. I quickly exited the car to return the hug, and I gave her a kiss. Predictably, she said I was skinny and needed to gain weight. I turned towards my brothers and my sister. We all smiled, then there was a moment of hesitation between us. They really didn't know me very well. I may have been the oldest kid in the family, but when I left for Mexico, my youngest brother Luke was only five years old. Annie was ten, Gary was thirteen, and Mark was fourteen. After a minute, we relaxed, and they gave me a hug. We'd have to get to know each other again.

We went into the house, everyone talking at once, asking me questions. I opened my backpack and took out my uh'ap (bowl) and pronounced the word. Then pulled out my ch'op (water jug) pronounced the word Then the *pixjola* (hat) and *qejch'* (a strap that goes over the forehead). All they wanted was for me to re-pronounce the names for those items. The language was so guttural, it made them laugh. I had pictures; taken with my old Kodak Instamatic 110 camera from a single roll of film, these were the only I took the whole time I was in Sitala. I reached deep into my backpack and pulled up a handful of *kajpej* (coffee). I pronounced the word in Tzeltal and told them I had picked the beans and used my *o'ejch* (coffee bag) to carry the beans down the muddy hillsides. They were silent. They could not grasp that I had been living in a place so primitive and foreign from the busy, Southern California life that was all they knew. This was beyond their imagination of what I'd been doing for two and a half years. They somehow thought I was living the same life they were, only in Mexico.

My father said he was going to Carl's Junior for hamburgers and fries, his favorite thing to do when the family gathered. If it wasn't hamburgers, it was donuts. I had not eaten American fast food in years, about an hour or so later, I was feeling a bit uncomfortable, hurried to the bathroom, and had diarrhea for the next two days. It had to have been the hamburger. I had mostly been eating whole foods for the last three years, my body totally rejected the heavily processed hamburger and fries. When I was eating food from the jungles of Chiapas and drinking untreated water from lakes and streams, I only suffered with diarrhea a few times and not nearly as bad as what I experienced eating a fast-food burger. I got over my gastronomical illness and took my time working back to an American diet. The conversation moved to diet, and I pulled up my uh'ap and explained that *uc'ohmacil,* a staple in the diet, was coarse cornmeal and a little sugar, mixed with water in the uh'ap and eaten with your index and middle finger. They got past that, but when I described eating bushmeat, monkey and snake they were disgusted. When I explained the many delicious fruits found in the rainforest, they were more relaxed.

After several days of talking and telling stories, we were ready to talk about my health. Mom said she had seen a seizure. I wasn't surprised and had suspected as much. I told her I thought I was having fewer seizures in Mexico. She understood that seizures were brought on by certain triggers and acknowledged that she now knew stress was a major cause. Mom said she understood now how much pressure I must have been under before I left for Mexico. She began telling me about an exciting possibility she had learned about.

My father's financial success, selling cardboard and paste board packaging, included lots of entertaining, dining, and drinking. One evening, at a cocktail party in Bel Aire, my mother was talking about me and shared my diagnosis of psycho-motor seizures with Dr. Paul Crandall, a neurosurgeon at the University of California-Los Angeles. Dr. Crandall's specialty was epilepsy, and he told my mother about a grant program at UCLA Neuropsychiatric Surgery Department studying frontal lobe seizures, and said he thought I might be a good candidate. Mom drove to UCLA the next day for a grant application and made an appointment for the following month. After my peaceful life in Chiapas, my seizures didn't seem as urgent to me anymore, but they were to my mother. I was a bit hesitant about starting a whole new medical treatment program that could involve surgery. I had never had surgery; I could understand surgery to repair a broken arm but not the brain. I could only visualize my head being shaved with a huge scar and wearing a hat for the rest of my life.

For thousands of years, the Mayans had been treating seizures using herbs and rituals by Shamans, balancing the human and animal spirits within us. I told Mom about this approach and suggested going back to Mexico for treatment there as an alternative. She looked at me in disbelief. She said, "No way are you going to be treated by a witchdoctor for seizures."

Mom shut that idea down quickly. I didn't argue any further and agreed to go to the consultation.

I nervously waited for the appointment, thinking about what might be next. I learned that the neuropsychiatric surgery department at UCLA was one of the best in the world. We would be seeing Dr. Crandall, the first doctor in the world to do long term EEG depth recording on a human brain. If accepted, I would become his twenty second patient.

Though my family was well off financially, we were not rich enough to bear the expense of a brain research program at UCLA. I wanted to discuss who was going to pay for this. My father said this was something that had to be worked out, but he was sure the grant would cover the expenses.

Chapter 20

UCLA or not?

Mom and Dad and I went together to the preliminary meeting. Passing through the door with a sign saying Neuro Psychiatric Surgery Center, I felt scared and out-of-place. The Shaman witchdoctors in the jungles of Chiapas were less frightening to me than this place. Even the smells of the Shaman caves with hundreds of herbs, bones, and ground up-insects was more pleasant than the sterile disinfectant smell of this medical center. I kept my chin up and walked forward with my parents at my side. We checked in and sat quietly in the waiting room wondering what would happen next. Then a side door opened, and a six-foot three, thin man in his fifties, wearing a white coat walked in. "Please follow me." It was Dr. Crandall; the man Mom had met at the cocktail party in Bel Aire.

We sat down on three overstuffed chairs across from his desk, and began describing the frequencies of my seizures, medications I'd taken, convulsions, and my awareness during and after seizures. He explained that the program was organized in three stages. The first would be working with a team of psychologists and neurologists. The second part was implanting sixteen electrodes into my brain. The implants would precisely identify from which part of the brain the seizures originated. If the doctors were successful in their identification, they would perform surgery to remove that portion of the brain. During Stage One, I would be in the hospital for two to three months of neurological and psychiatric testing. Stage Two, implanting the electrodes, would take another four months in the hospital, with more testing. Finally, there would be an additional three months for the surgery itself.

Dr. Crandall said that this surgery had only been done twenty-two times anywhere in the world. Not all surgeries had been fully successful, but all patients showed at least some improvement. There were many serious side effects that could emerge after the surgery, relating to speech, vision, and cognitive functioning such as memory and ability to learn. Some side effects were mild, others were not. There would be a break after the removal of the implants allowing my brain and skull to heal. Once the skull had healed, they would confirm the Third Stage, surgery, and I then would recover in the hospital for an additional three to four months. On average, the entire process took nine months. During the second and third stage, I would be under the care of two nurses twenty-four hours a day. They would be responsible for my well-being, not allowing me to fall or injure myself at any time while the electrodes were in my skull and after surgery.

The grant would also include extensive research of the brain during each step. Research included drug testing, participating in the development of both CAT and PERT radiology, and deep EEG experimentation.

The next opening for the grant would be in several months. They would notify me of my acceptance into the grant within one week, and then I would have ten days to decide.

My parents were most interested in the side effects. Fearing that this conversation might be too much for me, Dr. Crandall asked me to sit in the waiting room while he talked to them. I sat alone and fearful, thinking they were discussing terrible outcomes, brain damage, eyesight, language, and mobility difficulties. Leaving Dr. Crandall's office my parents looked confused, as if they couldn't quite believe what they'd just heard. The one-hour car ride home was unusually quiet.

Back home, we had the discussion about the many terrible side effects. Before we even finished the conversation I rushed to my room and buried my face in a pillow, thinking about everything that had happened in the last four and a half years, and how it now came to this enormous question. I lay there wondering if I might be better off gathering my things and heading back to Chiapas. I knew this was not a realistic fantasy: living in the rain forest as a Tzeltal Indian. In Mexico I had learned to be resilient, to get up and push forward under difficult circumstances. I remembered how I had gotten myself out of a Mexican jail, escaped after being held by witches, left a hospital with an injured leg, found food when hungry, and shelter when I was wet and cold, made friends when I was alone. I was scared and uncertain but reminded myself that I was capable of handling whatever might happen.

I ran downstairs, found my parents, and said, "I decided. I will do it."

My mother burst into tears and asked if, I was sure.

"Yes," I repeated, "I am sure."

Dad wasn't so sure. He worried about the possible side effects of the surgery and wanted us to talk more about them. Dr. Crandall had said I might not be able to speak, see, or walk again. I might have the demeanor of someone who'd had a lobotomy or suffer cognitive disabilities for the rest of my life. I said that would be stage three and we were not there yet. We sat quietly for a long time. Then I spoke up and said I felt so uncomfortable with the medication and the stigma surrounding me. I wanted to at least move forward with the first two stages of the grant. The following week, I received a letter saying that I was a good candidate and had been accepted into the program. I was excited to be approved but felt dazed and vulnerable about the risk I could be taking.

Up to this point, my siblings had been kept out of these conversations. I didn't feel that was fair. They were also concerned and worried about my well-being, so I explained what was going on, including Luke, although he was too young to understand. I knew Mom shielded them from the reality of my having an illness that was so hard to understand, and my father was protecting them from any stigma that they might encounter.

I gathered with them, without mom and dad, and explained that my years in Mexico had been one way to deal with my seizures, but now Mom had found a doctor who might be able to stop the seizures completely. We didn't talk about the side effects, but I gave them all the other information I had. I told them I would have to leave home again, and I wanted them to understand how hard it was for me being away. I assured them I would be close by and they could visit. They had so many questions. Will they cut your hair? Will you have a scar? Will it hurt? Many of which I could not answer. But they were unanimous in thinking I should go, and we promised to stay close. This conversation laid the foundation for the bond between us that has never wavered and has only become stronger over the years.

Chapter 21

The Hospital and Testing

Three weeks after the letter of acceptance arrived, I packed a suitcase, instead of my backpack, for the trip to UCLA, my new home for a while. When my parents and I arrived, the director of the grant program greeted us and took us to an upper floor, where I had a private room. She introduced us to one of the nurses, who gave me a gown to wear, even though I was not sick. After my parents received all the information they needed to stay in contact with me at the hospital, we stood together, our faces showing little emotion, then said good-bye.

The first night was lonely, the food was bland, and there was no one to talk to. The next morning, I was introduced to my nurses who were young and professional. They recognized that the gown I was wearing would probably be uncomfortable for all the locations in the hospital I would be going to, so they brought me a pair of surgical pants and a loose-fitting shirt.

One of the nurses and I reviewed my schedule for the next two weeks. In that first week, I met with a half a dozen psychologists who asked a million questions each. My experiences in Mexico astounded them. The testing began, and it was day after day, test after test: putting together story boards, ink blotter tests, memory tests, number tests, picture tests, general knowledge tests. Medical doctors came in to perform reflex tests, muscle tension tests, balance tests, and mobility tests. Things became more interesting when the vision tests began. They brought me down to a large room resembling an IMAX theater. The ceiling was a large white dome. I had a joystick with a button to push when dots appeared on the dome. This was not so easy, dots appearing so fast, no one could have pushed the button fast enough to capture them all. Then it was hearing tests. This testing went on all week. I felt sorry for my mom, as she tried to visit three or four times that first week, but I was never in my room. I was always somewhere else in the hospital being tested.

The second week at the hospital, they started a regimen of Electroencephagram, EEG testing, to measure the electrical activity in my brain. There were twenty wires connected to a huge computer which was cutting edge for its time, but one that would be considered ancient now. Each wire had a small metal pin on the end. Laying on a flat table, the EEG technician inserted the pin in my skull, which felt like a pinprick. Each test lasted longer than an hour. After a week of continuous EEG tests, they flashed lights and made loud noises to induce me to have seizures while connected to the EEG computer. Recognizing that I was getting tired after all this and could use a break, they gave me a few days off to recover. On one of the weekends, I had off from testing. My parents brought my siblings to the hospital. They did not stay long, but it was good to see them. I hoped their visit gave them a better understanding of what was happening to me. They snuck candy bars and shakes in for me.

The third week they repeated all the EEG tests from before, but this time, instead of inserting pins in my skull, they glued small metal disks to my scalp. After each test, they washed the glue out of my hair. I think my hair was washed ten times a day during that week. The second round of EEG testing seemed to be more for them than for me.

After about ten weeks of testing, my parents and I met with the psychiatrist, neurosurgeon, and neurologist. The doctors, lacking in bedside manner, spoke in a monotone, using unfamiliar scientific language. They had all the data they needed and had a good sense where to surgically implant the deep electrodes in my brain. The doctors needed another few weeks to further study and strategize the surgery and then I could go home for a short time before coming back for the electrode surgery. When I remembered this operation had been performed less than two dozen times, I knew I was truly a guinea pig.

Returning home to prepare myself for the implant surgery, extended family and friends started calling from all over the country to wish me luck. Friends of the family stopped by the house, asking what they could do, giving me pats on the back and assuring me everything would be alright. There was even a special mass at our Catholic church, Our Lady of Guadalupe, in my name. This encouragement came from people trying to be sympathetic and supportive, but most had absolutely no idea what I was going through. Hating to admit it to myself, I knew that this outpouring of goodwill was more tiring than the testing.

The support I received from Uncle Bill, who called from Brazil, helped the most. He emphasized how strong I was, reminding me to think about all the mountains I had climbed traveling through Mexico, learning new languages and living in a different culture. I cried, and I let him know I could have never had those experiences if it was not for him giving me the guidance and opportunity. When we finished our call, Uncle Bill told me BO'CONISH DE SA WILAB (good traveling) in Tzeltal.

With that, I was ready. I did my best to help my family relax and not worry. This was the first time in a while I had a genuine smile on my face. My attitude was positive and optimistic. I had decided the next mountain was waiting to be climbed.

But the smile left my face when I started thinking about how differently I'd grown up compared to my siblings and friends. I fell into a low level of depression, and I slept more, ate less, cried multiple times throughout the day, and interacted less with people. Living with a mental health condition, having epilepsy, and getting ready for experimental brain surgery, I admitted that my life may never be normal. People might always look at me as someone different. I found it impossible to talk to anyone about my real feelings. I kept it all inside, pretending I was alright, though, if I was truthful, I'd have to admit I was struggling.

The night before going back to the hospital, Mom fixed my favorite dinner, her special beef stroganoff, over rice. Then we returned to the weirdness of me living in the Psychiatric Neurosurgery ward at UCLA. We arrived before noon, meeting with Dr. Crandall in his office. He pulled out a full-size model of my skull, with sixteen holes drilled into it. He explained that these were the locations they would insert the gold electrodes into my brain. They used gold because of its purity and because of its ability to conduct electricity. He said my head would be shaved and after surgery I would have to wear a helmet at all times, more like a large turban around my head, to protect me from infection and the electrodes and from bumping the electrodes. He reminded me that two nurses would be with me wherever I went, including the bathroom. The nurses had only one job, to protect the electrodes from being displaced. I had never been escorted wherever I went, especially to the bathroom. I remembered being escorted to the edge of the green, soft, and moist Huautla forest by two Mazateca women wearing traditional clothing, preparing me to eat magic mushrooms. That was more peaceful and exciting than being escorted around a hospital with carts rolling in all directions and loud intercoms.

I watched sadly as my parents walked away, leaving me at the hospital. I went upstairs, changed out of my street clothes, put on a pair of surgical pants, went out into the hallway, and said hello to the nurses on the ward. The second time around was much more comfortable. Now I knew my way around the floor and even remembered where the ice cream was in the nurses' refrigerator.

Prepping for the surgery took several days. I met the surgical team, and my special bodyguard nurses. They measured me for a head support. The surgery was short, several hours. My head was shaven, and with a marking pen, they drew directly on my skull the location of each electrode. Sixteen holes total. During the drilling, I was asleep and only awakened for the insertion of the electrodes. I was in the Intensive Care Unit for two days after the surgery. My biggest enemy was the mirror. Every time I looked in the mirror, I saw a weird, alien type creature, and it was me. That was me. The protective gear I was wearing was the size of a beach ball. I had a special pillow, or head rest, that reminded me of wooden head supports I had seen in National Geographic magazine by African women who had extended their necks with metal rings. I slept on my back the entire time the electrodes were implanted. There I was, the ultimate freak laying in a hospital bed.

My parents couldn't visit for the two days I was in the ICU, but they were there the day I returned to my regular room. The size of my protective headgear surprised them. Of course, as always, mom showed me unconditional love. My father was a different story. Although he smiled at me, I think inside he was thinking, this can't be my child. When he asked me if I always had to wear "that thing" on my head, I knew he did not fully understand what was going on. The nurses came in, introduced themselves, and assured my parents they would be looking out for me every minute of the day. Mom and Dad didn't stay long that day, probably because my father needed time to digest what he saw. I wasn't ill, no blood, no fever, I was healthy, and I wanted to be treated as if I was healthy. After they left, I broke down crying several times and had difficulty sleeping that night. I was worried they wouldn't come back. I felt abandoned again.

The next morning, I woke up with the two nurses by my side. I went to the bathroom with two nurses by my side and took a shower with nurses by my side. There was no privacy, twenty-four seven. The doctors and technicians had me doing many of the same tests as before, but this time with small wires attached to the electrodes inserted into my brain. Countless vision, hearing, and cognitive tests went on for several more weeks. Dr. Martin, the lead neurologist on the team, explained to me that the EEG testing gave them an overall location. The deep implants would show them the precise area of the brain where the seizures originated from.

I was hesitant to see visitors because of their reaction to me: sometimes disbelief, and sometimes laughing. Laughing was the best and most relaxing. I laughed a lot around old friends, joking around suggesting that I would make a great skit on a comedy show. The joke was on me, but that was alright. I was the star of the moment. The worst visits were from friends of the family, neighbors, and when my friends would bring their boyfriend or girlfriend with them. They were always trying to be overly nice and tried to be encouraging without really understanding what empathy was. I knew I would scream if one more person told me they knew how I felt. They had no idea how I felt. Mom, my sister, and my brothers came frequently, usually three days per week. Dad came during his lunch hours and sometimes after work. I was glad when he came because he brought good snacks with him. Beef Jerky was my favorite. Since he was always in a suit and tie, he looked like he was on his last sales call of the day. He would want to know everything I had done that day, testing, and conversations with the doctors. Visits from dad differed from visits from mom. Dad, although loving, was more business-like, always wanting to know the details. Mon wanted to know how I was feeling.

The best visitor was my grandmother, Nana, the sweetest person I knew. She always brought edible gifts she made herself; if not cookies or brownies, it was a special candy she made from the figs growing in her backyard. She always made enough for the nurses too. The nurses were wonderful with visitors, always explained what they were doing and if I was up to it, they would break the rules and let visits last longer. If they saw I was tired and drifting off, they would step in and cut a visit short to spare me from awkwardly asking someone to leave.

The testing was tiring and was not entirely focused on my seizures. Since I already had the brain implants, they were doing marijuana tests, psychedelic drug testing and who knows what else. I went through so many brain-altering and out of my mind drug tests it was hard to keep track of all they were doing. But my environment felt secure, and I trusted the doctors, some of the best in the world. The marijuana tests were comical, the nurses and doctors had little or no experience smoking pot. They came into the exam room with a small amount of pot in a sterile jar and a small sterile laboratory pipe. They fumbled while loading the pipe, held the pipe up to my lips like they were feeding a baby, lit the pipe and said inhale, pulled back the pipe and said exhale, then fed it to me again. Never had I smoked marijuana in such a controlled and supervised environment. I did compliment them for having good pot.

I was always awake during testing, although often in a twilight type of sedation. Sometimes my arms and legs would start lifting and moving involuntarily because they were sending electrical impulses through the brain implants. I was a complete experimental subject. One day during the drug testing, they set up a series of strobe lights to flash in a pattern to induce seizures. The light show was good, perhaps too good since they managed to cause a grand mal seizure that day. I was grateful to be sedated that day having never experienced a grand mal seizure before.

The most unpleasant part was "The Chair." Part of the grant was experimenting with different methods of imaging the brain. This was new testing in the development of "computed axial tomography" or CAT scan, and the use of nuclear dyes in CAT and Pet scans. The CAT scan was invented in England in 1972. They invented the PET at UCLA in 1973. Both the CAT and PET scans were still in full development and experimentation when I was at UCLA, being used as a guinea pig. UCLA was still developing technology and methods to use CAT scans for better brain imaging using nuclear dyes.

In a large room, there were multiple pieces of x-ray equipment arranged in a circle, with a specialized chair in the middle. I would sit in this chair while it spun around inside the circle of twenty some x-ray machines, each one taking continuous pictures as I passed by. These experiments help lead to today's CAT scan, where the machine spins around the person, not the patient spinning around the machine.

I spun around the room in The Chair for hours, circling at different speeds, angles, and elevations. I sat for hours while they made hundreds of adjustments to the apparatus. It did not stop there. Nuclear dyes, an uncharted science in 1972 were used to help map my brain; I participated in their discovery.

Today, they deliver nuclear dyes intravenously. I had the dye injected through a spinal tap, which sent the dyes directly into my brain. Terrible headaches can occur if the patient moves during or after the spinal tap. This was a big problem because it was impossible for me not to move while revolving in a circle. The doctors had developed a pump mounted to my back that would inject the nuclear dye into the spinal cord while I was spinning. The headaches I got were so painful I would frequently vomit. When that happened, they stopped the testing long enough to give me morphine. As soon as the pain lessened, the tests started back. When the pain started again, they would stop and administer more morphine. The testing went on for hours, for many days. By the end of each day, drugged out of my mind with morphine, I was not able to even get out of bed. I told my parents, nurses, and the doctor that I couldn't go on with this testing. My parents met with my medical team where they learned more details about the CAT and PET testing. The research the hospital was doing was obviously more for the development of CAT and PET scans than my health. This part of grant testing stopped. Less than one year later, UCLA was credited with inventing the PET scan. Forty years later, I had an appointment with a neurologist in North Carolina.

We were discussing my medical history at UCLA when he asked, "Were you ever in the chair?"

He was a resident doctor at the UCLA hospital in the early 70s. He knew of Dr. Crandall and the foundation he was heading with the hospital researching epilepsy. We talked for another half hour about my experiences.

After a few days of break from the testing regimen, I was feeling like myself again and anxious to move around outside the hospital and get some fresh air. The nurses came up with a risky but fun idea: to go to the movies. UCLA is in Westwood, a college town full of student, teachers, restaurants, bookstores, theaters, and movies. The newest movie available was One Flew Over the Cuckoo's Nest, starring Jack. A movie based on the book by Ken Kesey. Jack Nicholson portrayed a mental patient in a poorly run psychiatric hospital, intent on saving other mental patients from the wrath of Nurse Ratchet, the worst nurse ever. I didn't know anything about the film but agreed to go.

The planning began. First, they needed some type of ethical clearance to take a patient from the psychiatric ward at the hospital to see a movie about a fictional mental patient in a fictional mental hospital. Second, how would we get there? The theater was within walking distance, but how could the nurses guarantee my safety since I was still having seizures? The doctors were not concerned that I would fall as much as that I would just wander off and bump my head. After all, I had sixteen gold electrodes protruding from my skull. The slightest collision with the electrodes would be a disaster. I didn't want to think about what could happen to me and my brain. The hospital contacted my parents, who said they agreed to letting me live in the jungles in the highlands of Chiapas, Mexico and there were no problems, so how could this be any more dangerous? We set a date for the following week. My biggest worry was my appearance. My head bandages were humongous, my skin was pale from living in a hospital, I was very thin, and I was a little unstable on my feet. I would be wearing the two-inch canvas belt, like a leash, that stroke and orthopedic patients wear so nurses can stabilize and prevent them from falling. For me to walk into a movie about a mental hospital would be like a person wearing a spacesuit walking into a Star Trek movie.

On the day of our outing, the two nurses and I started walking the four short blocks to the theater. This turned out to be a bigger ordeal than I expected. There was no disguising what we were doing. Wearing surgical pants and shirt, being escorted down the street in a busy city neighborhood tethered to two nurses. Everyone looked at me like this was some type of movie advertisement or theater prop. They gave me a thumbs up on my costume. At the theater, we had to stand in a will-call line to receive our tickets. Bumping into people was not a problem: people looked at me and the way I was standing, the same way I was taught to stand while waiting for the coffee to be picked in

Sitala and gave me all the space I needed. Once in the cinema, the usher agreed I needed a special seat, where people could see around me without having to stare at the back of my headgear.

The movie was fantastic. Jack Nicholson at his best, starting a rebellion in a mental hospital where patients were lobotomized to drooling zombies to control their behavior. We left with everyone staring, walked back to the hospital and called it a night.

Chapter 22

The Surgery

My parents received a call from Dr. Crandall. He said they had isolated the location where the seizures originated and that the team was confident it was operable. They recommended removing the electrodes and allowing three months for my skull to heal.

When we met with him again, in person, he explained in detail, using a model of the brain, how the electrode studies would guide him to the precise location where the seizures initiated. He would remove approximately two square inches of my brain, about the size of a baby's fist. But he would not perform the operation without my consent, since I was an adult. This was a dangerous, highly specialized surgery, called a frontal lobe lobectomy. If the operation did not go well, I could lose my speech, eyesight, memory, and or cognitive ability to learn. My parents did not want me to make an immediate decision. I also wanted more time think about it, and I wanted to know more about the outcomes of others who had had had the surgery. It turned out that their surgeries were only moderately successful. All recipients had a reduction in seizures, and several reported they were almost seizure-free.

Several individuals experienced side effects like patients who have received a full lobotomy, such as cognitive difficulties and some paralysis. I was frightened and undecided. After leaving Dr. Crandall's office, we returned to my hospital room looking at each other in silence. My two nurses stepped out of the room, knowing the importance of our meeting with the doctor, and sensing our current mood. It was one of the few times in months that they had given me complete privacy. I was sure they knew what we'd discussed with Dr. Crandall.

Mom and Dad left shortly afterward both of them giving me a kiss and saying we'd talk in the morning.

After a fitful night, I made my decision. I had come this far making risky choices in my life, and now I had to make another one. Living a life that felt like only a partial life, having to take anticonvulsant drugs and enduring seizures and the stigma surrounding epilepsy could be no worse than living with side effects of the surgery. Yes, the chances of being seizure-free, without any side effects, was a longshot, but I was convinced, even as my mind second-guessed my decision, that surgery was my best option. Although some friends of my parents, even a doctor they knew disagreed, no one tried to talk me out of it. It was my decision.

By the next morning it was obvious to me that all the nurses on the ward knew the decision I had made by hearing remarks such as "You can't leave us here all alone." "The ward will not be the same if you didn't return." The positive and caring response from everyone on the floor was so empathetic I started to cry. After so many months together we were like family. I shared Thanksgiving and Christmas in the hospital with them. They were positive about my decision and guaranteed their ongoing care and support when I returned for the surgery. The head nurse told me I could keep the key to the nurse's refrigerator until I returned. We scheduled the removal of the electrodes for the following week. I had many visits with doctors who would be involved in the operation, x-rays were taken of my skull allowing them to plan for the surgery over the next three months. The electrodes were removed, my head was bandaged, and I went home to wait.

Knowing that my best chance of a successful surgery was for my body to be in top condition. I resolved to eat right and exercise. Coming home was not like a homecoming from a surgery that had cured an illness. I came home to a family and friends who were worried about the surgery that lay ahead, and the possible outcome. I hated the constant sympathy, not empathy, people patting me on the back, losing their voices saying you will be all right. Talking about what I was feeling now would have felt better; it seemed like people were preparing me for the worst outcome rather than the best outcome. I started my regimen of exercise, a high-protein diet, and no partying for the next three months. I was dedicated, and I kept to my schedule.

One day I had to return to the hospital for an appointment, and I took time to go up to fourth floor, and say hello, and let them know how I was doing. One of the nurses suggested that I try yoga for relaxation. On our way home, we stopped by the library, where I selected several books on yoga, mindfulness, and meditation, which became my outlet and release for fear and anxiety. As I added meditation and mindfulness to my daily schedule, I felt a positive change in myself. I was careful to keep these practices to myself since these were new concepts to Americans then. The best way I understood these mind-driven exercises was to connect them to the work shamans did back in the highlands of Chiapas during a cleansing to clear one's mind prior to healing. My family would have had difficulty understanding how this all fit into brain surgery. They had a hard enough time understanding some of my experiences in Mexico.

I continued healthy living and exercise, running and throwing the medicine ball Uncle Bill had given me and my brothers years before. The best yoga position I found was the Deadman pose. Lying on my back, hands slightly cupped, slack jawed, eyes closed, I would think of the Shamans and witch doctors in the jungle using their powers to cleanse the mind and body of negativity and the struggle of human and animal spirits within, though of course I was not also using smoke, fire, herbs, and dancing. I became adept at putting myself into a trance-like state and floating away into a different peaceful mindset.

As surgery approached, there were more appointments with psychiatrists and psychologists making sure I was making the right decision for myself and not being directed or manipulated by others. The psychiatrists and neurologists didn't know what to think when I brought up my experiences with shamans and witch doctors, meditation, and mindfulness. It was 1972, and Western medicine had not yet caught up with the many alternative Eastern and Indian medicine practices.

The last week before I returned to UCLA, people started stopping by the house once again, even the Catholic priest from Our Lady of Guadalupe, our parish church. Uncle Mike, from Maryland, and Uncle Bill, from Brazil, called me. It felt good to have their support. I recognized that everyone was hoping for a positive outcome, but I could also sense their fears.

It was difficult leaving my siblings again. They hugged me before I got in the car with my parents. Then we backed out of the driveway for what would be a quiet one-hour drive to the hospital. We had talked about the surgery for so long there was nothing more to discuss a. The hospital team welcomed me back with smiles and positivity. I changed into my hospital attire, then gave my mom a big kiss and hug. She broke down in tears for the longest time. I hugged my father and gave him a strong handshake. Tears rolled down his cheek as well. At that moment, surrounded by my parents' love, I felt it would all work out.

The surgery wouldn't be for several more days, though I would have preferred if it was the next day. My nurses said the surgery would be ten to twelve hours. I had to be awake the entire time so that they could monitor different brain functions during surgery. Therefore, I would be in a deep twilight sedation, rather than general anesthesia. The brain has no nerve endings, so I would feel no pain in the brain itself. Of course, the anesthesiologist and many other assisting doctors wanted to meet me and repeat what the others had said. It always ended with, "I hope to see you again when this is over."

There was nothing I could say in response except, "I'll see you later."

On the day before surgery, I had dinner in the afternoon, and there would be no breakfast. At bedtime I put myself in the yoga Savasana pose and started to relax the way I had taught myself. The nurse came in to give me a pill to relax and sleep. I refused the medication and said I wanted to do this on my own. The nurse said she had to check with a doctor. A doctor came in and tried to explain why the medication was prescribed. I again refused and told the doctor they could sedate me for the surgery itself, but I wanted to prepare for it in my own way.

The next morning, they moved me from my bed to a surgical bed, where I lay back and again put my body in the Savasana pose. The gurney transport through the hospital corridors to surgery seemed like the longest trip I had ever taken. My face was aimed straight up and all I could see was the texture and pattern of the ceiling tile. I felt relaxed and confident this was going to work; I had spent the last three months preparing my mind and body for the surgery. Suddenly, I fell into the most beautiful mental state I had ever experienced, like I was on an air mattress floating down a cool, slow stream. I was thinking of death and never coming back after the surgery, and it did not seem bad or scary. I was totally relaxed, floating in calm, serene space.

The surgery took eleven hours. I was told the most difficult aspect of the surgery was keeping me awake.

I was asleep when they rolled me into the recovery room. When I came to, I opened my eyes and saw ten people, including my parents, staring down at me. Dr. Crandall looked at me and said, "Do you know where you are?"

I responded that I was in the UCLA Neuropsychiatric Surgery Center waiting to go to surgery. Dr. Crandall asked another five or six questions and finished by asking me the names of everyone in the room. I got every question right. Dr. Crandall raised his eyebrows, looked at the other doctors in the room, smiled, and said, "I haven't seen this before."

I pulled back the sheets on my bed and tried to get up. The staff held me back and said not to move until all the tubes were removed. I looked up at my parents. They had tears in their eyes.

The next morning, I sat up on the side of the hospital bed with assistance. I hadn't eaten anything in twenty-four hours besides Jell-O and ice chips, and I was hungry. I felt soreness at the horseshoe shaped incision on my head. IVs, catheters, and tubing were everywhere. A huge weight had been lifted off of my shoulders: I could talk, walk, and had not become a drooling zombie. Dr. Crandall came in and said that the surgery had gone well, and if I continued to do as well over the next few weeks, I could leave the hospital. My body was in good shape, and I was recovering quickly. The last week in the hospital seemed busier than ever, with doctors all over me, doing psychological and neurological testing all day long.

At the end of the week, my parents met with Dr. Crandall in his office. He said my skull and incision were healing fine, and that they had not observed any damaging side effects due to the surgery, nor any seizure activity. He paused, then said, "John, you are making a remarkable recovery. The outcome of the surgery has been the most successful this hospital has ever seen."

When finished praising me, I asked, "Am I seizure free?"

After a long pause, he said, "We have not seen in person, or in testing any seizures. In most cases, we have only seen patients have fewer seizures, not a complete absence of seizures. Maybe you will be the first. Your brain has a lot of healing to go through, so I don't want to say you will never have another seizure. We must wait and see."

I knew there was still healing that needed time, but I also knew now I was going to make it.

I was discharged from the hospital with the nurses and staff waving goodbye and wishing me the best. Back home sitting on the couch in the family room, with the bandages off my shaved skull revealing the long horseshoe incision on the right side of my head, I picked up a book. Trying to read, I discovered I could not track my eyes from sentence to sentence. My eyes just wandered the page. I called my mother who immediately called the hospital and made an appointment for the next morning. I met with an eye specialist. She said I'd lost some volunteer control of my eye movement, but that this condition could improve with therapy. Dr. Crandall contacted me and explained that this was a new side effect he had not seen. He referred me to an eye therapist. Therapy sessions began within a week and took place at home twice a week. I worked hard at these eye exercises for over three months, because it was important to me to read again. Eventually I regained the ability to keep my eye on the line I was reading. Still, reading was slower and not as enjoyable as it once had been. Eye exercises remained a daily activity for more than a year, when reading finally became normal again. As it turned out eye movement was the most serious side effect I had from the surgery.

Is this over? I had prepared myself for side effects that would have left me years of recovery from the surgery. Not the positive life informing side effects I gathered over the last five years traveling in Mexico. Learning to push forward without ever giving up, maybe slowing to a snail's pace, moving forward in baby steps, but never coming to a complete halt. Like climbing a steep mountain that seems impossible, never stopping, just taking smaller strides. The positive side effects of listening even when you don't speak the language. Watching when learning a new skill. Smiling while working no matter how difficult the task is. Using empathy not sympathy when in a conflict. The side effects of taking a risk, no matter how big the risk is to better your life. The risk I took paid off.

Epilogue

I have been free of seizures without medication for the last fifty years. Follow-up visits with the UCLA Neurosurgery doctors continued for ten years after the surgery. I went back to school and completed college with a focus on special education and human behavior. After college I worked at one of the first mainstreaming special education classrooms in California. One summer, I worked with a friend, building a boat, and rediscovered how much I enjoyed working with my hands. Woodworking became my passion for forty more years as I worked designing and building furniture. This obsession may have been a skill inherited from my grandfather, or it came from working with wood with the Tzeltal Indians building food stalls and shelters.

At thirty-one, I married Suzanne, a mixed media textile artist, the most creative woman I have ever met. With her two boys from a first marriage, six-year-old Jim and four-year-old Devin, we had an instant family. After we married, we had a son, Matthew. We now have three smart, handsome, and successful adult sons. Suzanne and I both ventured towards the arts, left California, and moved to Asheville, North Carolina, one of the most popular art destinations in the country. Asheville was our home for thirty years. We both had dual careers: me in construction management, home inspection, and furniture making: Suzanne as an accountant while developing her textile art business. We opened two art galleries showing contemporary craft, exhibiting my furniture and Suzanne's large scale woven art and framed mixed media art, along with many other professional craft artists. Now, we are both retired and living comfortably in Madison, Wisconsin.

After college, our older boys settled in the Midwest. Jim and Matthew, both in Madison, and Devin in Chicago. Jim and Devin are both married, and we have four wonderful grandchildren.

Post-surgery, my father and I never developed a close father son relationship. My father could not let go of years of disruption I caused him and the family. My dad had sent all my siblings to good colleges and universities. When I recovered, I asked my father if he would pay for my education as he did for my brothers and sister. His response was not what I expected, he turned to me and replied, "I have done enough for you."

I did not let this rejection keep us apart, and, until he died, I tried to keep our friendship as close as possible. Mom and I were very close and often talked about all I had gone through in my journey to wellness. My brothers and sister have stayed close all these years and remain my best friends. Uncle Bill's life with his new family in California became unsettled and ironically he moved to be close to me in Asheville, We stayed very close until he passed away at age eighty-five.

I like thinking back fifty years, traveling thousands of miles through Mexico then finding myself in

Chiapas picking coffee and living with and close to the Tzeltal and Lacondon people whose civilization was five hundred years behind mine. Volunteering my time at a medical clinic with a dirt floor assisting with surgeries and child birthing at the age of seventeen. Riding a mule alongside an amazingly gifted and giving mayor, priest, doctor, nurse and dedicated, kind and strong men through the highlands and jungles of southern Mexico.

Spending almost a year in a hospital, preparing for brain surgery. I was lucky to come out on the other side a new man. When I ask myself what have I learned about myself through all of this? I can look in the mirror and say you can be picked up and dropped off anywhere in the world under any condition. I will figure it out. I will be OK.

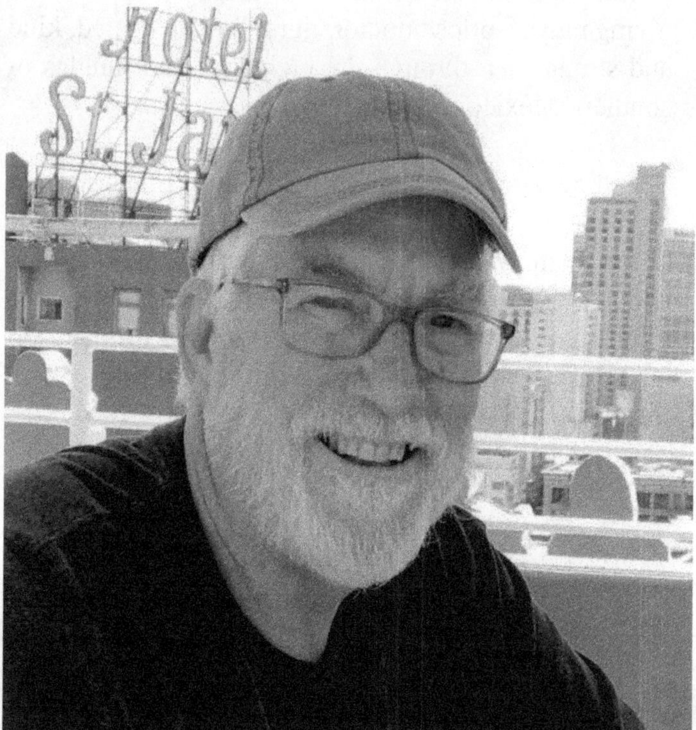
Hotel